C-509   CAREER EXAMINATION SERIES

*This is your
PASSBOOK for...*

Motorman

*Test Preparation Study Guide
Questions & Answers*

COPYRIGHT NOTICE

This book is SOLELY intended for, is sold ONLY to, and its use is RESTRICTED to individual, bona fide applicants or candidates who qualify by virtue of having seriously filed applications for appropriate license, certificate, professional and/or promotional advancement, higher school matriculation, scholarship, or other legitimate requirements of education and/or governmental authorities.

This book is NOT intended for use, class instruction, tutoring, training, duplication, copying, reprinting, excerption, or adaptation, etc., by:

1) Other publishers
2) Proprietors and/or Instructors of "Coaching" and/or Preparatory Courses
3) Personnel and/or Training Divisions of commercial, industrial, and governmental organizations
4) Schools, colleges, or universities and/or their departments and staffs, including teachers and other personnel
5) Testing Agencies or Bureaus
6) Study groups which seek by the purchase of a single volume to copy and/or duplicate and/or adapt this material for use by the group as a whole without having purchased individual volumes for each of the members of the group
7) Et al.

Such persons would be in violation of appropriate Federal and State statutes.

PROVISION OF LICENSING AGREEMENTS – Recognized educational, commercial, industrial, and governmental institutions and organizations, and others legitimately engaged in educational pursuits, including training, testing, and measurement activities, may address request for a licensing agreement to the copyright owners, who will determine whether, and under what conditions, including fees and charges, the materials in this book may be used them. In other words, a licensing facility exists for the legitimate use of the material in this book on other than an individual basis. However, it is asseverated and affirmed here that the material in this book CANNOT be used without the receipt of the express permission of such a licensing agreement from the Publishers. Inquiries re licensing should be addressed to the company, attention rights and permissions department.

All rights reserved, including the right of reproduction in whole or in part, in any form or by any means, electronic or mechanical, including photocopying, recording, or by any information storage and retrieval system, without permission in writing from the Publisher.

Copyright © 2024 by
National Learning Corporation

212 Michael Drive, Syosset, NY 11791
(516) 921-8888 • www.passbooks.com
E-mail: info@passbooks.com

PUBLISHED IN THE UNITED STATES OF AMERICA

PASSBOOK® SERIES

THE *PASSBOOK® SERIES* has been created to prepare applicants and candidates for the ultimate academic battlefield – the examination room.

At some time in our lives, each and every one of us may be required to take an examination – for validation, matriculation, admission, qualification, registration, certification, or licensure.

Based on the assumption that every applicant or candidate has met the basic formal educational standards, has taken the required number of courses, and read the necessary texts, the *PASSBOOK® SERIES* furnishes the one special preparation which may assure passing with confidence, instead of failing with insecurity. Examination questions – together with answers – are furnished as the basic vehicle for study so that the mysteries of the examination and its compounding difficulties may be eliminated or diminished by a sure method.

This book is meant to help you pass your examination provided that you qualify and are serious in your objective.

The entire field is reviewed through the huge store of content information which is succinctly presented through a provocative and challenging approach – the question-and-answer method.

A climate of success is established by furnishing the correct answers at the end of each test.

You soon learn to recognize types of questions, forms of questions, and patterns of questioning. You may even begin to anticipate expected outcomes.

You perceive that many questions are repeated or adapted so that you can gain acute insights, which may enable you to score many sure points.

You learn how to confront new questions, or types of questions, and to attack them confidently and work out the correct answers.

You note objectives and emphases, and recognize pitfalls and dangers, so that you may make positive educational adjustments.

Moreover, you are kept fully informed in relation to new concepts, methods, practices, and directions in the field.

You discover that you are actually taking the examination all the time: you are preparing for the examination by "taking" an examination, not by reading extraneous and/or supererogatory textbooks.

In short, this PASSBOOK®, used directedly, should be an important factor in helping you to pass your test.

MOTORMAN

DUTIES:
To be immediately responsible for the protection of passengers and the safety, regularity, proper care and operation of cars and trains in accordance with the rules, regulations, and special instructions governing employees engaged in operation, in performance of the following work depending on assignment: (1) operate trains in revenue service and between yards and terminals; (2) in yard or terminal service, switch cars, prepare trains for road service and operate trains between yards and terminals; (3) perform such other duties as the transit authority is authorized by law to prescribe in its regulations.

SCOPE OF TH EXAMINATION:
The written test will consist of multiple-choice questions and may include questions designed to determine the candidate's relative judgment and knowledge with respect to transit authority operating rules, regulations and procedures, train controls and car equipment; railroad signals; safety; emergency procedures and unusual conditions; duties of other transit personnel involved in train operations; and other related areas pertaining to the operation of trains.

HOW TO TAKE A TEST

I. YOU MUST PASS AN EXAMINATION

A. *WHAT EVERY CANDIDATE SHOULD KNOW*

Examination applicants often ask us for help in preparing for the written test. What can I study in advance? What kinds of questions will be asked? How will the test be given? How will the papers be graded?

As an applicant for a civil service examination, you may be wondering about some of these things. Our purpose here is to suggest effective methods of advance study and to describe civil service examinations.

Your chances for success on this examination can be increased if you know how to prepare. Those "pre-examination jitters" can be reduced if you know what to expect. You can even experience an adventure in good citizenship if you know why civil service exams are given.

B. *WHY ARE CIVIL SERVICE EXAMINATIONS GIVEN?*

Civil service examinations are important to you in two ways. As a citizen, you want public jobs filled by employees who know how to do their work. As a job seeker, you want a fair chance to compete for that job on an equal footing with other candidates. The best-known means of accomplishing this two-fold goal is the competitive examination.

Exams are widely publicized throughout the nation. They may be administered for jobs in federal, state, city, municipal, town or village governments or agencies.

Any citizen may apply, with some limitations, such as the age or residence of applicants. Your experience and education may be reviewed to see whether you meet the requirements for the particular examination. When these requirements exist, they are reasonable and applied consistently to all applicants. Thus, a competitive examination may cause you some uneasiness now, but it is your privilege and safeguard.

C. *HOW ARE CIVIL SERVICE EXAMS DEVELOPED?*

Examinations are carefully written by trained technicians who are specialists in the field known as "psychological measurement," in consultation with recognized authorities in the field of work that the test will cover. These experts recommend the subject matter areas or skills to be tested; only those knowledges or skills important to your success on the job are included. The most reliable books and source materials available are used as references. Together, the experts and technicians judge the difficulty level of the questions.

Test technicians know how to phrase questions so that the problem is clearly stated. Their ethics do not permit "trick" or "catch" questions. Questions may have been tried out on sample groups, or subjected to statistical analysis, to determine their usefulness.

Written tests are often used in combination with performance tests, ratings of training and experience, and oral interviews. All of these measures combine to form the best-known means of finding the right person for the right job.

II. HOW TO PASS THE WRITTEN TEST

A. NATURE OF THE EXAMINATION

To prepare intelligently for civil service examinations, you should know how they differ from school examinations you have taken. In school you were assigned certain definite pages to read or subjects to cover. The examination questions were quite detailed and usually emphasized memory. Civil service exams, on the other hand, try to discover your present ability to perform the duties of a position, plus your potentiality to learn these duties. In other words, a civil service exam attempts to predict how successful you will be. Questions cover such a broad area that they cannot be as minute and detailed as school exam questions.

In the public service similar kinds of work, or positions, are grouped together in one "class." This process is known as *position-classification*. All the positions in a class are paid according to the salary range for that class. One class title covers all of these positions, and they are all tested by the same examination.

B. FOUR BASIC STEPS

1) Study the announcement

How, then, can you know what subjects to study? Our best answer is: "Learn as much as possible about the class of positions for which you've applied." The exam will test the knowledge, skills and abilities needed to do the work.

Your most valuable source of information about the position you want is the official exam announcement. This announcement lists the training and experience qualifications. Check these standards and apply only if you come reasonably close to meeting them.

The brief description of the position in the examination announcement offers some clues to the subjects which will be tested. Think about the job itself. Review the duties in your mind. Can you perform them, or are there some in which you are rusty? Fill in the blank spots in your preparation.

Many jurisdictions preview the written test in the exam announcement by including a section called "Knowledge and Abilities Required," "Scope of the Examination," or some similar heading. Here you will find out specifically what fields will be tested.

2) Review your own background

Once you learn in general what the position is all about, and what you need to know to do the work, ask yourself which subjects you already know fairly well and which need improvement. You may wonder whether to concentrate on improving your strong areas or on building some background in your fields of weakness. When the announcement has specified "some knowledge" or "considerable knowledge," or has used adjectives like "beginning principles of..." or "advanced ... methods," you can get a clue as to the number and difficulty of questions to be asked in any given field. More questions, and hence broader coverage, would be included for those subjects which are more important in the work. Now weigh your strengths and weaknesses against the job requirements and prepare accordingly.

3) Determine the level of the position

Another way to tell how intensively you should prepare is to understand the level of the job for which you are applying. Is it the entering level? In other words, is this the position in which beginners in a field of work are hired? Or is it an intermediate or advanced level? Sometimes this is indicated by such words as "Junior" or "Senior" in the class title. Other jurisdictions use Roman numerals to designate the level – Clerk I, Clerk II, for example. The word "Supervisor" sometimes appears in the title. If the level is not indicated by the title, check the description of duties. Will you be working under very close supervision, or will you have responsibility for independent decisions in this work?

4) Choose appropriate study materials

Now that you know the subjects to be examined and the relative amount of each subject to be covered, you can choose suitable study materials. For beginning level jobs, or even advanced ones, if you have a pronounced weakness in some aspect of your training, read a modern, standard textbook in that field. Be sure it is up to date and has general coverage. Such books are normally available at your library, and the librarian will be glad to help you locate one. For entry-level positions, questions of appropriate difficulty are chosen – neither highly advanced questions, nor those too simple. Such questions require careful thought but not advanced training.

If the position for which you are applying is technical or advanced, you will read more advanced, specialized material. If you are already familiar with the basic principles of your field, elementary textbooks would waste your time. Concentrate on advanced textbooks and technical periodicals. Think through the concepts and review difficult problems in your field.

These are all general sources. You can get more ideas on your own initiative, following these leads. For example, training manuals and publications of the government agency which employs workers in your field can be useful, particularly for technical and professional positions. A letter or visit to the government department involved may result in more specific study suggestions, and certainly will provide you with a more definite idea of the exact nature of the position you are seeking.

III. KINDS OF TESTS

Tests are used for purposes other than measuring knowledge and ability to perform specified duties. For some positions, it is equally important to test ability to make adjustments to new situations or to profit from training. In others, basic mental abilities not dependent on information are essential. Questions which test these things may not appear as pertinent to the duties of the position as those which test for knowledge and information. Yet they are often highly important parts of a fair examination. For very general questions, it is almost impossible to help you direct your study efforts. What we can do is to point out some of the more common of these general abilities needed in public service positions and describe some typical questions.

1) General information

Broad, general information has been found useful for predicting job success in some kinds of work. This is tested in a variety of ways, from vocabulary lists to questions about current events. Basic background in some field of work, such as sociology or economics, may be sampled in a group of questions. Often these are principles which have become familiar to most persons through exposure rather than through formal training. It is difficult to advise you how to study for these questions; being alert to the world around you is our best suggestion.

2) Verbal ability

An example of an ability needed in many positions is verbal or language ability. Verbal ability is, in brief, the ability to use and understand words. Vocabulary and grammar tests are typical measures of this ability. Reading comprehension or paragraph interpretation questions are common in many kinds of civil service tests. You are given a paragraph of written material and asked to find its central meaning.

3) Numerical ability

Number skills can be tested by the familiar arithmetic problem, by checking paired lists of numbers to see which are alike and which are different, or by interpreting charts and graphs. In the latter test, a graph may be printed in the test booklet which you are asked to use as the basis for answering questions.

4) Observation

A popular test for law-enforcement positions is the observation test. A picture is shown to you for several minutes, then taken away. Questions about the picture test your ability to observe both details and larger elements.

5) Following directions

In many positions in the public service, the employee must be able to carry out written instructions dependably and accurately. You may be given a chart with several columns, each column listing a variety of information. The questions require you to carry out directions involving the information given in the chart.

6) Skills and aptitudes

Performance tests effectively measure some manual skills and aptitudes. When the skill is one in which you are trained, such as typing or shorthand, you can practice. These tests are often very much like those given in business school or high school courses. For many of the other skills and aptitudes, however, no short-time preparation can be made. Skills and abilities natural to you or that you have developed throughout your lifetime are being tested.

Many of the general questions just described provide all the data needed to answer the questions and ask you to use your reasoning ability to find the answers. Your best preparation for these tests, as well as for tests of facts and ideas, is to be at your physical and mental best. You, no doubt, have your own methods of getting into an exam-taking mood and keeping "in shape." The next section lists some ideas on this subject.

IV. KINDS OF QUESTIONS

Only rarely is the "essay" question, which you answer in narrative form, used in civil service tests. Civil service tests are usually of the short-answer type. Full instructions for answering these questions will be given to you at the examination. But in case this is your first experience with short-answer questions and separate answer sheets, here is what you need to know:

1) Multiple-choice Questions

Most popular of the short-answer questions is the "multiple choice" or "best answer" question. It can be used, for example, to test for factual knowledge, ability to solve problems or judgment in meeting situations found at work.

A multiple-choice question is normally one of three types—
- It can begin with an incomplete statement followed by several possible endings. You are to find the one ending which *best* completes the statement, although some of the others may not be entirely wrong.
- It can also be a complete statement in the form of a question which is answered by choosing one of the statements listed.

- It can be in the form of a problem – again you select the best answer.

Here is an example of a multiple-choice question with a discussion which should give you some clues as to the method for choosing the right answer:

When an employee has a complaint about his assignment, the action which will *best* help him overcome his difficulty is to
   A. discuss his difficulty with his coworkers
   B. take the problem to the head of the organization
   C. take the problem to the person who gave him the assignment
   D. say nothing to anyone about his complaint

In answering this question, you should study each of the choices to find which is best. Consider choice "A" – Certainly an employee may discuss his complaint with fellow employees, but no change or improvement can result, and the complaint remains unresolved. Choice "B" is a poor choice since the head of the organization probably does not know what assignment you have been given, and taking your problem to him is known as "going over the head" of the supervisor. The supervisor, or person who made the assignment, is the person who can clarify it or correct any injustice. Choice "C" is, therefore, correct. To say nothing, as in choice "D," is unwise. Supervisors have and interest in knowing the problems employees are facing, and the employee is seeking a solution to his problem.

2) True/False Questions

The "true/false" or "right/wrong" form of question is sometimes used. Here a complete statement is given. Your job is to decide whether the statement is right or wrong.

SAMPLE: A roaming cell-phone call to a nearby city costs less than a non-roaming call to a distant city.

This statement is wrong, or false, since roaming calls are more expensive.
This is not a complete list of all possible question forms, although most of the others are variations of these common types. You will always get complete directions for answering questions. Be sure you understand *how* to mark your answers – ask questions until you do.

V. RECORDING YOUR ANSWERS

Computer terminals are used more and more today for many different kinds of exams.
For an examination with very few applicants, you may be told to record your answers in the test booklet itself. Separate answer sheets are much more common. If this separate answer sheet is to be scored by machine – and this is often the case – it is highly important that you mark your answers correctly in order to get credit.
An electronic scoring machine is often used in civil service offices because of the speed with which papers can be scored. Machine-scored answer sheets must be marked with a pencil, which will be given to you. This pencil has a high graphite content which responds to the electronic scoring machine. As a matter of fact, stray dots may register as answers, so do not let your pencil rest on the answer sheet while you are pondering the correct answer. Also, if your pencil lead breaks or is otherwise defective, ask for another.

Since the answer sheet will be dropped in a slot in the scoring machine, be careful not to bend the corners or get the paper crumpled.

The answer sheet normally has five vertical columns of numbers, with 30 numbers to a column. These numbers correspond to the question numbers in your test booklet. After each number, going across the page are four or five pairs of dotted lines. These short dotted lines have small letters or numbers above them. The first two pairs may also have a "T" or "F" above the letters. This indicates that the first two pairs only are to be used if the questions are of the true-false type. If the questions are multiple choice, disregard the "T" and "F" and pay attention only to the small letters or numbers.

Answer your questions in the manner of the sample that follows:

32. The largest city in the United States is
 A. Washington, D.C.
 B. New York City
 C. Chicago
 D. Detroit
 E. San Francisco

1) Choose the answer you think is best. (New York City is the largest, so "B" is correct.)
2) Find the row of dotted lines numbered the same as the question you are answering. (Find row number 32)
3) Find the pair of dotted lines corresponding to the answer. (Find the pair of lines under the mark "B.")
4) Make a solid black mark between the dotted lines.

VI. BEFORE THE TEST

Common sense will help you find procedures to follow to get ready for an examination. Too many of us, however, overlook these sensible measures. Indeed, nervousness and fatigue have been found to be the most serious reasons why applicants fail to do their best on civil service tests. Here is a list of reminders:

- Begin your preparation early – Don't wait until the last minute to go scurrying around for books and materials or to find out what the position is all about.
- Prepare continuously – An hour a night for a week is better than an all-night cram session. This has been definitely established. What is more, a night a week for a month will return better dividends than crowding your study into a shorter period of time.
- Locate the place of the exam – You have been sent a notice telling you when and where to report for the examination. If the location is in a different town or otherwise unfamiliar to you, it would be well to inquire the best route and learn something about the building.
- Relax the night before the test – Allow your mind to rest. Do not study at all that night. Plan some mild recreation or diversion; then go to bed early and get a good night's sleep.
- Get up early enough to make a leisurely trip to the place for the test – This way unforeseen events, traffic snarls, unfamiliar buildings, etc. will not upset you.
- Dress comfortably – A written test is not a fashion show. You will be known by number and not by name, so wear something comfortable.

- Leave excess paraphernalia at home – Shopping bags and odd bundles will get in your way. You need bring only the items mentioned in the official notice you received; usually everything you need is provided. Do not bring reference books to the exam. They will only confuse those last minutes and be taken away from you when in the test room.
- Arrive somewhat ahead of time – If because of transportation schedules you must get there very early, bring a newspaper or magazine to take your mind off yourself while waiting.
- Locate the examination room – When you have found the proper room, you will be directed to the seat or part of the room where you will sit. Sometimes you are given a sheet of instructions to read while you are waiting. Do not fill out any forms until you are told to do so; just read them and be prepared.
- Relax and prepare to listen to the instructions
- If you have any physical problem that may keep you from doing your best, be sure to tell the test administrator. If you are sick or in poor health, you really cannot do your best on the exam. You can come back and take the test some other time.

VII. AT THE TEST

The day of the test is here and you have the test booklet in your hand. The temptation to get going is very strong. Caution! There is more to success than knowing the right answers. You must know how to identify your papers and understand variations in the type of short-answer question used in this particular examination. Follow these suggestions for maximum results from your efforts:

1) Cooperate with the monitor
The test administrator has a duty to create a situation in which you can be as much at ease as possible. He will give instructions, tell you when to begin, check to see that you are marking your answer sheet correctly, and so on. He is not there to guard you, although he will see that your competitors do not take unfair advantage. He wants to help you do your best.

2) Listen to all instructions
Don't jump the gun! Wait until you understand all directions. In most civil service tests you get more time than you need to answer the questions. So don't be in a hurry. Read each word of instructions until you clearly understand the meaning. Study the examples, listen to all announcements and follow directions. Ask questions if you do not understand what to do.

3) Identify your papers
Civil service exams are usually identified by number only. You will be assigned a number; you must not put your name on your test papers. Be sure to copy your number correctly. Since more than one exam may be given, copy your exact examination title.

4) Plan your time
Unless you are told that a test is a "speed" or "rate of work" test, speed itself is usually not important. Time enough to answer all the questions will be provided, but this does not mean that you have all day. An overall time limit has been set. Divide the total time (in minutes) by the number of questions to determine the approximate time you have for each question.

5) Do not linger over difficult questions

If you come across a difficult question, mark it with a paper clip (useful to have along) and come back to it when you have been through the booklet. One caution if you do this – be sure to skip a number on your answer sheet as well. Check often to be sure that you have not lost your place and that you are marking in the row numbered the same as the question you are answering.

6) Read the questions

Be sure you know what the question asks! Many capable people are unsuccessful because they failed to *read* the questions correctly.

7) Answer all questions

Unless you have been instructed that a penalty will be deducted for incorrect answers, it is better to guess than to omit a question.

8) Speed tests

It is often better NOT to guess on speed tests. It has been found that on timed tests people are tempted to spend the last few seconds before time is called in marking answers at random – without even reading them – in the hope of picking up a few extra points. To discourage this practice, the instructions may warn you that your score will be "corrected" for guessing. That is, a penalty will be applied. The incorrect answers will be deducted from the correct ones, or some other penalty formula will be used.

9) Review your answers

If you finish before time is called, go back to the questions you guessed or omitted to give them further thought. Review other answers if you have time.

10) Return your test materials

If you are ready to leave before others have finished or time is called, take ALL your materials to the monitor and leave quietly. Never take any test material with you. The monitor can discover whose papers are not complete, and taking a test booklet may be grounds for disqualification.

VIII. EXAMINATION TECHNIQUES

1) Read the general instructions carefully. These are usually printed on the first page of the exam booklet. As a rule, these instructions refer to the timing of the examination; the fact that you should not start work until the signal and must stop work at a signal, etc. If there are any *special* instructions, such as a choice of questions to be answered, make sure that you note this instruction carefully.

2) When you are ready to start work on the examination, that is as soon as the signal has been given, read the instructions to each question booklet, underline any key words or phrases, such as *least, best, outline, describe* and the like. In this way you will tend to answer as requested rather than discover on reviewing your paper that you *listed without describing*, that you selected the *worst* choice rather than the *best* choice, etc.

3) If the examination is of the objective or multiple-choice type – that is, each question will also give a series of possible answers: A, B, C or D, and you are called upon to select the best answer and write the letter next to that answer on your answer paper – it is advisable to start answering each question in turn. There may be anywhere from 50 to 100 such questions in the three or four hours allotted and you can see how much time would be taken if you read through all the questions before beginning to answer any. Furthermore, if you come across a question or group of questions which you know would be difficult to answer, it would undoubtedly affect your handling of all the other questions.

4) If the examination is of the essay type and contains but a few questions, it is a moot point as to whether you should read all the questions before starting to answer any one. Of course, if you are given a choice – say five out of seven and the like – then it is essential to read all the questions so you can eliminate the two that are most difficult. If, however, you are asked to answer all the questions, there may be danger in trying to answer the easiest one first because you may find that you will spend too much time on it. The best technique is to answer the first question, then proceed to the second, etc.

5) Time your answers. Before the exam begins, write down the time it started, then add the time allowed for the examination and write down the time it must be completed, then divide the time available somewhat as follows:
   - If 3-1/2 hours are allowed, that would be 210 minutes. If you have 80 objective-type questions, that would be an average of 2-1/2 minutes per question. Allow yourself no more than 2 minutes per question, or a total of 160 minutes, which will permit about 50 minutes to review.
   - If for the time allotment of 210 minutes there are 7 essay questions to answer, that would average about 30 minutes a question. Give yourself only 25 minutes per question so that you have about 35 minutes to review.

6) The most important instruction is to *read each question* and make sure you know what is wanted. The second most important instruction is to *time yourself properly* so that you answer every question. The third most important instruction is to *answer every question*. Guess if you have to but include something for each question. Remember that you will receive no credit for a blank and will probably receive some credit if you write something in answer to an essay question. If you guess a letter – say "B" for a multiple-choice question – you may have guessed right. If you leave a blank as an answer to a multiple-choice question, the examiners may respect your feelings but it will not add a point to your score. Some exams may penalize you for wrong answers, so in such cases *only*, you may not want to guess unless you have some basis for your answer.

7) Suggestions
   a. Objective-type questions
      1. Examine the question booklet for proper sequence of pages and questions
      2. Read all instructions carefully
      3. Skip any question which seems too difficult; return to it after all other questions have been answered
      4. Apportion your time properly; do not spend too much time on any single question or group of questions

5. Note and underline key words – *all, most, fewest, least, best, worst, same, opposite*, etc.
6. Pay particular attention to negatives
7. Note unusual option, e.g., unduly long, short, complex, different or similar in content to the body of the question
8. Observe the use of "hedging" words – *probably, may, most likely*, etc.
9. Make sure that your answer is put next to the same number as the question
10. Do not second-guess unless you have good reason to believe the second answer is definitely more correct
11. Cross out original answer if you decide another answer is more accurate; do not erase until you are ready to hand your paper in
12. Answer all questions; guess unless instructed otherwise
13. Leave time for review

b. Essay questions
1. Read each question carefully
2. Determine exactly what is wanted. Underline key words or phrases.
3. Decide on outline or paragraph answer
4. Include many different points and elements unless asked to develop any one or two points or elements
5. Show impartiality by giving pros and cons unless directed to select one side only
6. Make and write down any assumptions you find necessary to answer the questions
7. Watch your English, grammar, punctuation and choice of words
8. Time your answers; don't crowd material

8) Answering the essay question

Most essay questions can be answered by framing the specific response around several key words or ideas. Here are a few such key words or ideas:

M's: manpower, materials, methods, money, management
P's: purpose, program, policy, plan, procedure, practice, problems, pitfalls, personnel, public relations

a. Six basic steps in handling problems:
1. Preliminary plan and background development
2. Collect information, data and facts
3. Analyze and interpret information, data and facts
4. Analyze and develop solutions as well as make recommendations
5. Prepare report and sell recommendations
6. Install recommendations and follow up effectiveness

b. Pitfalls to avoid
1. *Taking things for granted* – A statement of the situation does not necessarily imply that each of the elements is necessarily true; for example, a complaint may be invalid and biased so that all that can be taken for granted is that a complaint has been registered

2. *Considering only one side of a situation* – Wherever possible, indicate several alternatives and then point out the reasons you selected the best one
3. *Failing to indicate follow up* – Whenever your answer indicates action on your part, make certain that you will take proper follow-up action to see how successful your recommendations, procedures or actions turn out to be
4. *Taking too long in answering any single question* – Remember to time your answers properly

IX. AFTER THE TEST

Scoring procedures differ in detail among civil service jurisdictions although the general principles are the same. Whether the papers are hand-scored or graded by machine we have described, they are nearly always graded by number. That is, the person who marks the paper knows only the number – never the name – of the applicant. Not until all the papers have been graded will they be matched with names. If other tests, such as training and experience or oral interview ratings have been given, scores will be combined. Different parts of the examination usually have different weights. For example, the written test might count 60 percent of the final grade, and a rating of training and experience 40 percent. In many jurisdictions, veterans will have a certain number of points added to their grades.

After the final grade has been determined, the names are placed in grade order and an eligible list is established. There are various methods for resolving ties between those who get the same final grade – probably the most common is to place first the name of the person whose application was received first. Job offers are made from the eligible list in the order the names appear on it. You will be notified of your grade and your rank as soon as all these computations have been made. This will be done as rapidly as possible.

People who are found to meet the requirements in the announcement are called "eligibles." Their names are put on a list of eligible candidates. An eligible's chances of getting a job depend on how high he stands on this list and how fast agencies are filling jobs from the list.

When a job is to be filled from a list of eligibles, the agency asks for the names of people on the list of eligibles for that job. When the civil service commission receives this request, it sends to the agency the names of the three people highest on this list. Or, if the job to be filled has specialized requirements, the office sends the agency the names of the top three persons who meet these requirements from the general list.

The appointing officer makes a choice from among the three people whose names were sent to him. If the selected person accepts the appointment, the names of the others are put back on the list to be considered for future openings.

That is the rule in hiring from all kinds of eligible lists, whether they are for typist, carpenter, chemist, or something else. For every vacancy, the appointing officer has his choice of any one of the top three eligibles on the list. This explains why the person whose name is on top of the list sometimes does not get an appointment when some of the persons lower on the list do. If the appointing officer chooses the second or third eligible, the No. 1 eligible does not get a job at once, but stays on the list until he is appointed or the list is terminated.

X. HOW TO PASS THE INTERVIEW TEST

The examination for which you applied requires an oral interview test. You have already taken the written test and you are now being called for the interview test – the final part of the formal examination.

You may think that it is not possible to prepare for an interview test and that there are no procedures to follow during an interview. Our purpose is to point out some things you can do in advance that will help you and some good rules to follow and pitfalls to avoid while you are being interviewed.

What is an interview supposed to test?

The written examination is designed to test the technical knowledge and competence of the candidate; the oral is designed to evaluate intangible qualities, not readily measured otherwise, and to establish a list showing the relative fitness of each candidate – as measured against his competitors – for the position sought. Scoring is not on the basis of "right" and "wrong," but on a sliding scale of values ranging from "not passable" to "outstanding." As a matter of fact, it is possible to achieve a relatively low score without a single "incorrect" answer because of evident weakness in the qualities being measured.

Occasionally, an examination may consist entirely of an oral test – either an individual or a group oral. In such cases, information is sought concerning the technical knowledges and abilities of the candidate, since there has been no written examination for this purpose. More commonly, however, an oral test is used to supplement a written examination.

Who conducts interviews?

The composition of oral boards varies among different jurisdictions. In nearly all, a representative of the personnel department serves as chairman. One of the members of the board may be a representative of the department in which the candidate would work. In some cases, "outside experts" are used, and, frequently, a businessman or some other representative of the general public is asked to serve. Labor and management or other special groups may be represented. The aim is to secure the services of experts in the appropriate field.

However the board is composed, it is a good idea (and not at all improper or unethical) to ascertain in advance of the interview who the members are and what groups they represent. When you are introduced to them, you will have some idea of their backgrounds and interests, and at least you will not stutter and stammer over their names.

What should be done before the interview?

While knowledge about the board members is useful and takes some of the surprise element out of the interview, there is other preparation which is more substantive. It *is* possible to prepare for an oral interview – in several ways:

1) Keep a copy of your application and review it carefully before the interview

This may be the only document before the oral board, and the starting point of the interview. Know what education and experience you have listed there, and the sequence and dates of all of it. Sometimes the board will ask you to review the highlights of your experience for them; you should not have to hem and haw doing it.

2) Study the class specification and the examination announcement

Usually, the oral board has one or both of these to guide them. The qualities, characteristics or knowledges required by the position sought are stated in these documents. They offer valuable clues as to the nature of the oral interview. For example, if the job involves supervisory responsibilities, the announcement will usually indicate that knowledge of modern supervisory methods and the qualifications of the candidate as a supervisor will be tested. If so, you can expect such questions, frequently in the form of a hypothetical situation which you are expected to solve. NEVER go into an oral without knowledge of the duties and responsibilities of the job you seek.

3) Think through each qualification required

Try to visualize the kind of questions you would ask if you were a board member. How well could you answer them? Try especially to appraise your own knowledge and background in each area, *measured against the job sought*, and identify any areas in which you are weak. Be critical and realistic – do not flatter yourself.

4) Do some general reading in areas in which you feel you may be weak

For example, if the job involves supervision and your past experience has NOT, some general reading in supervisory methods and practices, particularly in the field of human relations, might be useful. Do NOT study agency procedures or detailed manuals. The oral board will be testing your understanding and capacity, not your memory.

5) Get a good night's sleep and watch your general health and mental attitude

You will want a clear head at the interview. Take care of a cold or any other minor ailment, and of course, no hangovers.

What should be done on the day of the interview?

Now comes the day of the interview itself. Give yourself plenty of time to get there. Plan to arrive somewhat ahead of the scheduled time, particularly if your appointment is in the fore part of the day. If a previous candidate fails to appear, the board might be ready for you a bit early. By early afternoon an oral board is almost invariably behind schedule if there are many candidates, and you may have to wait. Take along a book or magazine to read, or your application to review, but leave any extraneous material in the waiting room when you go in for your interview. In any event, relax and compose yourself.

The matter of dress is important. The board is forming impressions about you – from your experience, your manners, your attitude, and your appearance. Give your personal appearance careful attention. Dress your best, but not your flashiest. Choose conservative, appropriate clothing, and be sure it is immaculate. This is a business interview, and your appearance should indicate that you regard it as such. Besides, being well groomed and properly dressed will help boost your confidence.

Sooner or later, someone will call your name and escort you into the interview room. *This is it.* From here on you are on your own. It is too late for any more preparation. But remember, you asked for this opportunity to prove your fitness, and you are here because your request was granted.

What happens when you go in?

The usual sequence of events will be as follows: The clerk (who is often the board stenographer) will introduce you to the chairman of the oral board, who will introduce you to the other members of the board. Acknowledge the introductions before you sit down. Do not be surprised if you find a microphone facing you or a stenotypist sitting by. Oral interviews are usually recorded in the event of an appeal or other review.

Usually the chairman of the board will open the interview by reviewing the highlights of your education and work experience from your application – primarily for the benefit of the other members of the board, as well as to get the material into the record. Do not interrupt or comment unless there is an error or significant misinterpretation; if that is the case, do not hesitate. But do not quibble about insignificant matters. Also, he will usually ask you some question about your education, experience or your present job – partly to get you to start talking and to establish the interviewing "rapport." He may start the actual questioning, or turn it over to one of the other members. Frequently, each member undertakes the questioning on a particular area, one in which he is perhaps most competent, so you can expect each member to participate in the examination. Because time is limited, you may also expect some rather abrupt switches in the direction the questioning takes, so do not be upset by it. Normally, a board member will not pursue a single line of questioning unless he discovers a particular strength or weakness.

After each member has participated, the chairman will usually ask whether any member has any further questions, then will ask you if you have anything you wish to add. Unless you are expecting this question, it may floor you. Worse, it may start you off on an extended, extemporaneous speech. The board is not usually seeking more information. The question is principally to offer you a last opportunity to present further qualifications or to indicate that you have nothing to add. So, if you feel that a significant qualification or characteristic has been overlooked, it is proper to point it out in a sentence or so. Do not compliment the board on the thoroughness of their examination – they have been sketchy, and you know it. If you wish, merely say, "No thank you, I have nothing further to add." This is a point where you can "talk yourself out" of a good impression or fail to present an important bit of information. Remember, *you close the interview yourself.*

The chairman will then say, "That is all, Mr. _____, thank you." Do not be startled; the interview is over, and quicker than you think. Thank him, gather your belongings and take your leave. Save your sigh of relief for the other side of the door.

How to put your best foot forward

Throughout this entire process, you may feel that the board individually and collectively is trying to pierce your defenses, seek out your hidden weaknesses and embarrass and confuse you. Actually, this is not true. They are obliged to make an appraisal of your qualifications for the job you are seeking, and they want to see you in your best light. Remember, they must interview all candidates and a non-cooperative candidate may become a failure in spite of their best efforts to bring out his qualifications. Here are 15 suggestions that will help you:

1) Be natural – Keep your attitude confident, not cocky

If you are not confident that you can do the job, do not expect the board to be. Do not apologize for your weaknesses, try to bring out your strong points. The board is interested in a positive, not negative, presentation. Cockiness will antagonize any board member and make him wonder if you are covering up a weakness by a false show of strength.

2) Get comfortable, but don't lounge or sprawl

Sit erectly but not stiffly. A careless posture may lead the board to conclude that you are careless in other things, or at least that you are not impressed by the importance of the occasion. Either conclusion is natural, even if incorrect. Do not fuss with your clothing, a pencil or an ashtray. Your hands may occasionally be useful to emphasize a point; do not let them become a point of distraction.

3) Do not wisecrack or make small talk

This is a serious situation, and your attitude should show that you consider it as such. Further, the time of the board is limited – they do not want to waste it, and neither should you.

4) Do not exaggerate your experience or abilities
In the first place, from information in the application or other interviews and sources, the board may know more about you than you think. Secondly, you probably will not get away with it. An experienced board is rather adept at spotting such a situation, so do not take the chance.

5) If you know a board member, do not make a point of it, yet do not hide it
Certainly you are not fooling him, and probably not the other members of the board. Do not try to take advantage of your acquaintanceship – it will probably do you little good.

6) Do not dominate the interview
Let the board do that. They will give you the clues – do not assume that you have to do all the talking. Realize that the board has a number of questions to ask you, and do not try to take up all the interview time by showing off your extensive knowledge of the answer to the first one.

7) Be attentive
You only have 20 minutes or so, and you should keep your attention at its sharpest throughout. When a member is addressing a problem or question to you, give him your undivided attention. Address your reply principally to him, but do not exclude the other board members.

8) Do not interrupt
A board member may be stating a problem for you to analyze. He will ask you a question when the time comes. Let him state the problem, and wait for the question.

9) Make sure you understand the question
Do not try to answer until you are sure what the question is. If it is not clear, restate it in your own words or ask the board member to clarify it for you. However, do not haggle about minor elements.

10) Reply promptly but not hastily
A common entry on oral board rating sheets is "candidate responded readily," or "candidate hesitated in replies." Respond as promptly and quickly as you can, but do not jump to a hasty, ill-considered answer.

11) Do not be peremptory in your answers
A brief answer is proper – but do not fire your answer back. That is a losing game from your point of view. The board member can probably ask questions much faster than you can answer them.

12) Do not try to create the answer you think the board member wants
He is interested in what kind of mind you have and how it works – not in playing games. Furthermore, he can usually spot this practice and will actually grade you down on it.

13) Do not switch sides in your reply merely to agree with a board member
Frequently, a member will take a contrary position merely to draw you out and to see if you are willing and able to defend your point of view. Do not start a debate, yet do not surrender a good position. If a position is worth taking, it is worth defending.

14) Do not be afraid to admit an error in judgment if you are shown to be wrong
The board knows that you are forced to reply without any opportunity for careful consideration. Your answer may be demonstrably wrong. If so, admit it and get on with the interview.

15) Do not dwell at length on your present job
The opening question may relate to your present assignment. Answer the question but do not go into an extended discussion. You are being examined for a *new* job, not your present one. As a matter of fact, try to phrase ALL your answers in terms of the job for which you are being examined.

Basis of Rating

Probably you will forget most of these "do's" and "don'ts" when you walk into the oral interview room. Even remembering them all will not ensure you a passing grade. Perhaps you did not have the qualifications in the first place. But remembering them will help you to put your best foot forward, without treading on the toes of the board members.

Rumor and popular opinion to the contrary notwithstanding, an oral board wants you to make the best appearance possible. They know you are under pressure – but they also want to see how you respond to it as a guide to what your reaction would be under the pressures of the job you seek. They will be influenced by the degree of poise you display, the personal traits you show and the manner in which you respond.

ABOUT THIS BOOK

This book contains tests divided into Examination Sections. Go through each test, answering every question in the margin. We have also attached a sample answer sheet at the back of the book that can be removed and used. At the end of each test look at the answer key and check your answers. On the ones you got wrong, look at the right answer choice and learn. Do not fill in the answers first. Do not memorize the questions and answers, but understand the answer and principles involved. On your test, the questions will likely be different from the samples. Questions are changed and new ones added. If you understand these past questions you should have success with any changes that arise. Tests may consist of several types of questions. We have additional books on each subject should more study be advisable or necessary for you. Finally, the more you study, the better prepared you will be. This book is intended to be the last thing you study before you walk into the examination room. Prior study of relevant texts is also recommended. NLC publishes some of these in our Fundamental Series. Knowledge and good sense are important factors in passing your exam. Good luck also helps. So now study this Passbook, absorb the material contained within and take that knowledge into the examination. Then do your best to pass that exam.

EXAMINATION SECTION

EXAMINATION SECTION
TEST 1

DIRECTIONS: Each question or incomplete statement is followed by several suggested answers or completions. Select the one that BEST answers the question or completes the statement. *PRINT THE LETTER OF THE CORRECT ANSWER IN THE SPACE AT THE RIGHT.*

Questions 1-12.

DIRECTIONS: Questions 1 through 12 apply to R-10 through R-42 cars.

1. The controls for the main car body lights of a train operate from
    A. 600 volts DC
    B. 120 volts AC
    C. a 32-volt battery
    D. a 600-volt battery

2. The color of the needle on the duplex air gauge that indicates straight air pipe pressure is
    A. black   B. blue   C. green   D. red

3. Dynamic braking is initiated by operation of the brake valve after moving the master controller handle to the _____ position.
    A. off   B. *multiple*   C. *switching*   D. *series*

4. On ME-42 brake valve type equipment, the brake valve handle can be removed when it is in the *handle off* position.
   In order to raise the brake valve handle so that it can be placed in the *handle off* position, it must FIRST be placed in the _____ position.
    A. running release
    B. full release
    C. full service
    D. emergency

5. When the brake valve handle is in the *running release* position, the brake pipe pressure should be _____ pounds.
    A. 0   B. 50   C. 72 to 80   D. 110

6. When the ME-42 brake valve handle is in the furthest position on the left, it is in the _____ position.
    A. full release
    B. handle off
    C. emergency
    D. full service

7. When a motorman leaves one operating station to go to another, the motorman should place the master controller handle in the *off* position and the reverser key in the _____ position.
    A. forward   B. reverse   C. thru   D. center

8. Two red lights will be displayed on both ends of the train when the reverser key is in the _____ position.
    A. center   B. multiple   C. forward   D. reverse

9. The speed of a train is increased by resistance automatically being cut out step by step when the master con-troller is in the _____ position.

   A. switching   B. multiple   C. set   D. forward

10. When a train is put into operation at a yard, a motorman must go through a sequence of steps before moving the train. One of the steps is to place the brake valve handle in the *full service* position.
    In this position, the train can not be moved until the duplex air gauge reads AT LEAST _____ pounds brake pipe pressure and _____ pounds straight air pipe pressure.

    A. 30; 50   B. 70; 110   C. 90; 70   D. 110; 70

11. The brake pipe angle cock is painted

    A. black   B. yellow   C. green   D. red

12. On married pair cars, batteries are provided on

    A. even-numbered cars only
    B. odd-numbered cars only
    C. each car
    D. none of the cars

13. Inverters are used on R-42 cars to supply power for the

    A. main fluorescent lights
    B. traction motors
    C. car heaters
    D. electric brakes

14. Contact shoe slippers are used

    A. as a replacement for contact shoes
    B. to provide an electrical connection with the contact rail
    C. as insulators
    D. when making the move from a BMT to an IRT line

15. When one contact shoe of a train car is touching the contact rail, the number of live shoes on that car is

    A. 1   B. 2   C. 4   D. 8

16. Motormen who are on duty are permitted to wear tinted glasses

    A. in the tunnels after a transit authority physician has examined them
    B. in the open, during daylight hours only
    C. only if they also carry a pair of untinted glasses
    D. at no time

17. The route request telephone located at a home signal is connected DIRECTLY to the

    A. desk trainmaster's office
    B. local tower
    C. crew dispatcher's office
    D. train dispatcher's office

18. One indication of weak storage batteries on a subway car is

    A. improper heater operation
    B. dim car body lights

C. dim headlights
D. improper fan operation

19. The term *single tracking* means that

    A. trains are operating in both directions on the same track
    B. all trains are operating on the local track
    C. there is skip-stop service
    D. all trains are operating on the express track

20. An employee who is NOT authorized to flag a train past a home signal that is indicating stop is a

    A. motorman instructor   B. trackman
    C. signal maintainer   D. towerman

21. When connecting a third rail emergency jumper to a train car shoe, it is IMPORTANT to

    A. connect the jumper to the third rail first
    B. connect the jumper to the car contact shoe first
    C. connect the jumper to the third rail and the car contact shoe at the same time
    D. use a contact shoe slipper

22. Motormen are responsible for information posted on the bulletin board.
    Of the following, the information LEAST likely to be found on a bulletin board is

    A. General Orders
    B. Employee Daily Work Assignments
    C. Train Schedules
    D. Official notices

23. A track frog is part of a

    A. curve   B. guard rail
    C. turnout   D. super elevated track

Questions 24-33.

DIRECTIONS: Questions 24 through 33 are based on the system of signal indications that is used on the BMT and IND and most of the IRT.

24. A signal whose aspect is controlled ONLY by the movement of a train is called a(n) _____ signal.

    A. marker   B. dwarf   C. home   D. automatic

25. A signal that gives ONLY a stop and stay indication is a(n) _____ signal.

    A. automatic   B. marker   C. home   D. dwarf

26. The signal aspect which means proceed on main route and be prepared to stop at the next signal is

    A. green over green   B. yellow over green
    C. green over yellow   D. yellow over yellow

27. When a train order signal displays two horizontal red lights, it is an indication to the motorman to

    A. stop and press the route request button
    B. call the command center
    C. remove the train from service
    D. proceed

28. The signal aspect which indicates that the motorman should stop and operate the automatic stop manual release is

    A. red over red
    B. yellow over yellow
    C. red over red over yellow
    D. yellow over yellow over yellow

29. When a signal displays a yellow over yellow over yellow, the motorman may be permitted to

    A. enter the inspection shed with caution
    B. stop and then operate the route request push button
    C. proceed with caution onto the yard lead
    D. stop and then operate the automatic stop manual release

30. When an approach signal displays a red over lunar white, the motorman should

    A. proceed on the diverging route and be prepared to stop at the next signal
    B. travel at a predetermined speed in order to clear the signal
    C. call the trainmaster
    D. close in on the preceding train

31. Of the following, the one that is NOT connected with time controlled signals is

    A. D   B. S   C. GF   D. GT

32. A signal used for slow speed movements only is called a(n) _____ signal.

    A. automatic   B. home   C. dwarf   D. marker

33. When the gap fillers are not sufficiently withdrawn to clear the sides of the cars, the gap filler signal displays a(n)

    A. yellow aspect
    B. red aspect
    C. illuminated sign bearing the letters GF
    D. white aspect

34. A repeater signal is used to repeat the indication of another signal. It is located on the _____ side of the track _____ the signal it repeats and has _____ automatic stop.

    A. same; as; an   B. same; as; no
    C. opposite; from; an   D. opposite; from; no

35. A sign bearing the letter *P* is connected with a(n)

    A. time controlled signal
    B. interlocking area
    C. employee loading platform
    D. power gap

36. A no clearance area along the subway's right of way is indicated by a sign that

    A. is all red
    B. has blue and white diagonal stripes
    C. has blue and yellow diagonal stripes
    D. has red and white diagonal stripes

37. The sign shown at the right with white letters against a green background is a _____ sign.
    A. reverse movement car stop
    B. resume speed
    C. station car stop
    D. reduce speed

38. The sign shown at the right means _____, allowable speed 15 M.P.H.
    A. derail
    B. diverging route
    C. distance repeater
    D. downgrade

39. A revenue train is a train that is used for

    A. picking up money collected by railroad clerks
    B. carrying passengers
    C. collecting garbage
    D. transporting lost articles

40. If a train is approaching a river tube from which dense smoke is coming, the motorman should

    A. ask the desk trainmaster whether he should enter the tube
    B. discuss entering the tube with the conductor
    C. not enter the tube under any condition
    D. unload passengers immediately

KEY (CORRECT ANSWERS)

1. C	11. A	21. B	31. C
2. D	12. A	22. C	32. C
3. A	13. A	23. C	33. B
4. D	14. C	24. D	34. D
5. D	15. C	25. B	35. C
6. A	16. B	26. B	36. D
7. D	17. B	27. B	37. B
8. A	18. C	28. C	38. B
9. B	19. A	29. C	39. A
10. C	20. B	30. B	40. C

TEST 2

DIRECTIONS: Each question or incomplete statement is followed by several suggested answers or completions. Select the one that BEST answers the question or completes the statement. *PRINT THE LETTER OF THE CORRECT ANSWER IN THE SPACE AT THE RIGHT.*

1. If a motorman loses the power to his train while traveling between stations, he should   1.____

   A. immediately apply his brakes into emergency
   B. try to coast to the next station
   C. check that the main knife switches are closed
   D. try to coast to an emergency alarm

2. A motorman must perform a rolling test before moving a train from a yard. The purpose of this test is to check that the   2.____

   A. hand brakes are operating properly
   B. dynamic brake is operating properly
   C. electro-pneumatic brakes release properly
   D. electro-pneumatic brakes can stop the train

3. The train buzzer signal consisting of two short buzzes   3.____

   A. is an answer to any signal
   B. means that the motorman should signal for a road car inspector
   C. means that the motorman should signal for a signal maintainer
   D. means proceed

4. The train buzzer signal consisting of three short buzzes means that the   4.____

   A. motorman should signal for a signal maintainer
   B. train has run by the station platform
   C. motorman should signal for a road car inspector
   D. motorman should apply the brakes instantly

5. The train buzzer signal consisting of two long buzzes means   5.____

   A. proceed
   B. stop
   C. that the motorman should sound the train horn for assistance
   D. that the train has run by the station platform

6. The train horn signal consisting of one long, one short, one long, one short, blast means   6.____

   A. stop
   B. that the train crew needs assistance
   C. that the train is making an irregular movement through the station
   D. that the motorman needs a signal maintainer

7. A succession of short blasts from a train horn could mean   7.____

   A. an alarm to persons on or near the track
   B. that the train is answering a signal

C. that the train needs a road car inspector
D. that the train has stopped short of the station platform

8. The tower horn signal consisting of one long, one short, blast means that the

   A. road car inspector should contact the tower
   B. trains in the interlocking limits should proceed
   C. train has taken the wrong route
   D. signal maintainer should contact the tower

9. When a motorman has removed power from a section of track, the ONLY one authorized to restore power is the

   A. same motorman
   B. safety officer
   C. power department supervisor
   D. desk trainmaster

10. A motorman can determine which is the signal rail on a track by

    A. inspecting the bond at the rail joint
    B. checking the position of the signal in the vicinity of the rail joint
    C. checking the position of the automatic stop in the vicinity of the rail joint
    D. checking the direction of normal train traffic

11. A train buzzer signal will sound at locations where the drum switch is in the _____ position.

    A. full release   B. thru
    C. off   D. release

12. According to the rules, a motorman is required to report any change of address within _____ days.

    A. two   B. three   C. five   D. seven

13. In the course of performing his duties, a motorman should have the LEAST need for

    A. train schedules   B. general orders
    C. train register sheets D. work programs

14. The standard gauge of track is the measurement of the distance between the _____ surfaces of the _____ of the rails.

    A. inside; base   B. outside; base
    C. inside; head   D. outside; head

15. The term *end incline* refers to the

    A. outside rail being raised above the inside rail
    B. portion of the car body end which extends beyond the normal line of clearance on curved tracks
    C. sloped approach to the third rail at gaps
    D. portion of the car body center which extends beyond the normal line of clearance on curved tracks

16. A flexible schedule is put into use PRIMARILY because of a(n)

    A. decision by the desk trainmaster to maintain a nonuniform headway
    B. interruption in service
    C. unusually heavy rush hour
    D. drag being transferred from one place to another

17. It is LEAST desirable to move an injured man before the arrival of a doctor if the man has

    A. first degree burns
    B. been internally injured
    C. a severe nosebleed
    D. been overcome from smoke

18. When a motorman is leaving an area under flagging protection, the last flagging light he should see is a _____ light.

    A. green   B. white   C. yellow   D. red

19. The indication to a motorman that there are men working on an adjacent track is _____ light(s).

    A. 2 yellow   B. 3 yellow   C. 1 red   D. 1 white

20. When a flagman moves a yellow light up and down, it USUALLY is an indication to the motorman that

    A. he can resume normal speed
    B. he must stop
    C. there is another flagman beyond
    D. there is a signal failure

21. Certain IRT transfer car and other miscellaneous work equipment are equipped with diversion valves.
    These diversion valves control the air to the

    A. supply reservoir   B. main reservoir
    C. trip cocks   D. compressor

22. Motormen assigned to road service must be on their trains at a terminal AT LEAST _____ minute(s) before their scheduled departure time.

    A. one   B. two   C. three   D. five

23. If a motorman's 10 car train is stopped on the road and he is told that power will be off for 30 minutes or more, he must apply the handbrakes.
    The handbrakes must be applied on a MINIMUM of _____ cars of his train.

    A. 2   B. 3   C. 4   D. 5

24. When a train leaves a terminal late, a motorman should

    A. try to close the gap, provided it can be done safely
    B. never try to close the gap because it is an unsafe practice
    C. close the gap before he reaches the other terminal
    D. ask the desk trainmaster whether he should try to close the gap

25. When a motorman overruns a station platform, he should back up the train

    A. if the desk trainmaster permits it
    B. if there is a flagman available to do the necessary flagging
    C. under no circumstances
    D. during rush hours only

26. Motormen are not allowed to bring containers of coffee into the operating cabs of the R-44 cars.
    The MAIN reason for this is that spilling the coffee can

    A. burn a motorman
    B. damage the electrical wiring
    C. dirty the cab
    D. affect a motorman's performance

27. On R-44 cars, the color of the light on the motorman's console that indicates that an end door is unlocked is

    A. red   B. white   C. yellow   D. blue

28. When a motorman sees a red automatic signal ahead, he must stop his train about 15 feet short of the signal. If the signal remains red and the motorman observes a train ahead, he should call the command center for instructions after waiting _____ minutes.

    A. two   B. five   C. seven   D. ten

29. The radio transceiver at a fixed wayside location that acts as a relay station for a fixed area is called a

    A. control center   B. mobile radio unit
    C. base station   D. portable transceiver

30. A train moving at the rate of 24 miles per hour will travel 4 miles in _____ minutes.

    A. 6   B. 10   C. 20   D. 96

31. Under normal conditions, when an R-44 train is ready to leave the terminal, the conductor should give the proceed signal to the motorman by

    A. the buzzer system
    B. the indicator
    C. voice on the train intercom
    D. the *proceed light*

32. If passengers are walking on the roadway without permission, it is MOST important to

    A. pull the emergency alarm
    B. call the transit police
    C. try to convince the passengers to get on a train
    D. call the safety department

33. A motorman discovers after his train has left the terminal that he must cut out a number of air brakes.
   The train may continue in passenger service if the brakes have been cut out on No more than _____ of the cars, none of which is an end car.

   A. 2/3   B. 1/2   C. 1/3   D. 1/4

34. When a train cannot move under its own power, the following train may be coupled to it if both have the same type of coupler.
   Under NO conditions should these trains be coupled

   A. electrically
   B. mechanically
   C. with a motorman in other than the front car
   D. pneumatically

35. When a motorman uncouples a car from a train and moves it backwards, the car must NOT be moved backwards more than _____ foot (feet).

   A. one   B. two   C. three   D. five

36. When a motorman is moving his train into a shop, he must NOT move faster than _____ mph.

   A. 1   B. 2   C. 5   D. 10

37. When a flagman is giving a proceed signal while an automatic signal shows stop, the motorman should

   A. proceed very slowly
   B. proceed at normal speed
   C. proceed looking closely at the track ahead
   D. stop and question the flagman

38. When coupling cars together, a motorman must make several stops before contact is made with the standing car.
   In good weather, the distance of the first stop from the standing car should be AT LEAST

   A. 3 car lengths   B. 2 car lengths
   C. 50 feet   D. 10 feet

39. A train is being laid up on a grade.
   The handbrakes should be applied on

   A. the downgrade end of the train on as many cars as necessary
   B. the upgrade end of the train on as many cars as necessary
   C. both ends of the train on as many cars as necessary
   D. all cars of the train so as to provide maximum safety

40. When a train is skipping a station, it must NOT go faster than _____ mph while passing the station platform.

   A. 3   B. 5   C. 10   D. 15

KEY (CORRECT ANSWERS)

1.	B	11.	C	21.	C	31.	C
2.	C	12.	D	22.	B	32.	A
3.	A	13.	C	23.	D	33.	C
4.	C	14.	C	24.	A	34.	A
5.	A	15.	C	25.	C	35.	A
6.	B	16.	B	26.	B	36.	C
7.	A	17.	B	27.	A	37.	D
8.	D	18.	A	28.	D	38.	B
9.	D	19.	B	29.	C	39.	A
10.	A	20.	C	30.	B	40.	D

EXAMINATION SECTION
TEST 1

DIRECTIONS: Each question or incomplete statement is followed by several suggested answers or completions. Select the one that BEST answers the question or completes the statement. *PRINT THE LETTER OF THE CORRECT ANSWER IN THE SPACE AT THE RIGHT.*

Questions 1-17.

DIRECTIONS: Questions 1 through 17 apply to R-10 to R-42 cars except where otherwise noted in the question.

1. When the brake pipe angle cock is open, its handle is

    A. pushed in all the way
    B. pulled out all the way
    C. turned to the right
    D. turned to the left

    1._____

2. When uncoupling cars, the straight air pipe pressure must be built up to a reading of AT LEAST _____ lbs.

    A. 72   B. 90   C. 105   D. 135

    2._____

3. The dynamic brakes on a car operate by means of

    A. the traction motors operating as generators
    B. the regular brake shoes on both trucks
    C. a second set of brake shoes on the #1 truck only
    D. hydraulic action

    3._____

4. When isolating a car in the middle of a train and cutting out its brakes, it is NECESSARY to close the

    A. brake pipe and straight air pipe angle cocks on both ends of the car
    B. brake pipe angle cocks on both ends of the car and leave the straight air pipe angle cocks open
    C. straight air pipe angle cocks on both ends of the car and leave the brake pipe angle cocks open
    D. brake pipe angle cock and the straight air pipe angle cock on the trouble end of the car only

    4._____

5. On R-42 cars, a converter is used

    A. in the load sensor system for controlling emergency brake applications
    B. in place of conventional motor generator sets
    C. in the traction motor drive system
    D. when moving from IND tracks to IRT tracks

    5._____

6. On married pair cars, compressors are provided on

    A. each car
    B. leading cars *only*
    C. even-numbered cars *only*
    D. odd-numbered cars *only*

    6._____

7. Battery power is used to provide energy for the

   A. heaters and fans
   B. main car lights
   C. door control circuit
   D. air compressors

8. Third rail power is used to provide energy for the

   A. train public address system
   B. electric brake
   C. motorman's indication
   D. side destination signs

9. When a motorman has moved the ME-42 brake valve handle to its furthest position on the right, he has placed the handle in the _____ position.

   A. emergency
   B. handle off
   C. full release
   D. full service

10. The CORRECT order of positions for the master controller from left to right in the cab is:

    A. Series - multiple - switching - off
    B. Series - switching - multiple - off
    C. Multiple - switching - series - off
    D. Multiple - series - switching - off

11. The B2 fuse or circuit breaker is in an electric circuit which affects the operation of the

    A. doors
    B. main lights
    C. traction motors
    D. brakes

12. The number of running positions for the master controller is

    A. 1   B. 2   C. 3   D. 4

13. When the brake valve handle is in the running release position, the straight air pipe pressure should be _____ pounds.

    A. 0   B. 50   C. 72 to 80   D. 110

14. The switching position on the master controller is used

    A. for short distance car movements, such as when coupling cars together
    B. when the motorman switches his operating position to another car
    C. for prolonged slow speed movements
    D. as the first running position

15. The direction in which a train moves is controlled PRIMARILY by the

    A. master controller
    B. reverser key
    C. main knife switch
    D. unit switch

16. The slowest running position of the master controller is the _____ position.

    A. parallel   B. switching   C. series   D. multiple

17. When a guard light on a car is lit, it indicates that 17.____

    A. the emergency brake valve on this car has been pulled
    B. the emergency brake valve on this car is in the normal position
    C. a door on the car is not properly closed or locked
    D. all doors on the car are properly closed and locked

Questions 18-24.

DIRECTIONS: Questions 18 through 24 are based on the system of signal aspect indications in use on Division B (BMT and IND) and most of Division A (IRT).

18. The signal aspect which means *proceed on diverging route* is 18.____

    A. green over green   B. yellow over green
    C. green over yellow   D. yellow over yellow

19. The signal aspect which means *proceed on diverging route prepared to stop at next signal* is 19.____

    A. yellow over green
    B. green over yellow
    C. yellow over yellow
    D. yellow over yellow over yellow

20. The signal aspect for a call-on is 20.____

    A. red over red over red
    B. red over red over yellow
    C. red over yellow over yellow
    D. yellow over yellow over yellow

21. An automatic signal displaying a yellow aspect means 21.____

    A. proceed on diverging route
    B. proceed on diverging route prepared to stop at next signal
    C. proceed prepared to stop at next signal
    D. approach at allowable speed

22. Depending on its type, a marker signal is equipped to show either a 22.____

    A. red aspect or a red over red aspect
    B. yellow aspect or a yellow over green aspect
    C. yellow or a red aspect
    D. green, a yellow, or a red and lunar white aspect

23. The signal aspect which means *approach at allowable speed then continue on main route* is 23.____

    A. green over green over yellow
    B. yellow over green over yellow
    C. yellow with an illuminated D signal
    D. yellow over green with an illuminated S signal

24. In the case of a signal displaying a green over green aspect, the lower green light indicates to a motorman

    A. to proceed
    B. that his train will take the main route
    C. that his train will take the diverging route
    D. a repeat of the upper green light

25. This sign indicates the
    A. beginning of a grade timing section where the allowable speed is 10 mph
    B. beginning of a grade timing section for 10 car trains
    C. end of a grade timing section, resume speed of 10 mph
    D. end of a grade timing section, resume speed for 10 car trains

26. This sign is a
    A. reverse movement car stop sign
    B. resume speed sign
    C. time control sign for R-type cars
    D. station car stop sign

27. A signal shows a switch is set for an express train to leave its schedule route and enter the local track while continuing on the same line. However, the motorman has not been previously informed about this change.
    In this case, the motorman

    A. must stop and call the desk trainmaster before proceeding
    B. must stop and call the towerman before proceeding
    C. must stop and signal for a signal maintainer before proceeding
    D. may proceed on the local track without obtaining permission or assistance

28. When a motorman sees a red automatic signal ahead, he must stop his train about 15 feet short of the signal, or at the yellow marker on the third rail protection board.
    The reason for doing this is to

    A. make sure the motorman is in position to use the lever, button, or special key to make the stop arm go down if necessary
    B. avoid passing the signal and not being able to see it when it changes to a yellow aspect
    C. make sure the insulated joint has been passed so as to allow the signal to change to a yellow aspect
    D. avoid passing the insulated joint so as to allow the signal to change to a yellow aspect

29. Home signals are USUALLY located at the entrance to all

    A. time control areas   B. routes
    C. stations   D. shops in yards

30. When the gap fillers are extended at a station so equipped, the gap filler signal will display a(n) 30.____

    A. illuminated sign bearing the letters GF and the track designation
    B. green aspect
    C. amber aspect
    D. red aspect

31. The buzzer signal which means *train has run by or stopped short of station platform* is _____ buzz(es). 31.____

    A. three short
    B. four short
    C. two long, two short
    D. one long, one short, one long, one short

32. It is NOT necessary for a motorman to receive two long buzzer signals from the conductor when starting a train 32.____

    A. at a terminal
    B. at a gap station
    C. after an emergency stop
    D. after cars have been added or cut

33. It is NOT necessary for a motorman to receive two long buzzer signals from the conductor when starting a train 33.____

    A. at a terminal
    B. at a gap station
    C. after an emergency stop
    D. after cars have been added or cut

34. The train whistle or horn signal which means *signal maintainer respond to train* is _____ blast(s). 34.____

    A. one short, one long   B. one long, one short
    C. four short   D. four long

35. The train whistle or horn signal which means *train request to towerman or switchmen for route or signal* is _____ blasts. 35.____

    A. two long   B. three short
    C. four short   D. four long

36. A tower horn signal consisting of one long blast means 36.____

    A. road car inspector contact tower
    B. all trains in the interlocking limits proceed at reduced speed
    C. all trains in the interlocking limits come to an immediate stop
    D. signal maintainer contact tower

37. The tower horn signal at an interlocking that means *trains in the interlocking limits proceed* is _____ blast(s). 37.____

    A. one long   B. one short
    C. two long   D. two short

38. Under normal flagging conditions, moving a white light up and down slowly is a signal to a motorman to proceed

    A. at a speed not to exceed 5 mph
    B. very slowly, prepared to stop within range of vision
    C. very slowly, prepared to stop within range of vision, and indicates that there is another flagman beyond
    D. at normal speed, prepared to stop at the next flagman if necessary

39. When an automatic signal is displaying a yellow aspect, the next automatic signal up ahead on the roadway at the same time will MOST likely be displaying a _____ aspect.

    A. green   B. yellow   C. red   D. blank

40. When a motorman is signaled by a flagman to stop his train, the motorman must stop the train at least _____ from the flagman.

    A. 1 car length   B. 2 car lengths
    C. 25 feet   D. 100 feet

KEY (CORRECT ANSWERS)

1. A	11. D	21. C	31. A
2. C	12. B	22. A	32. C
3. A	13. A	23. D	33. B
4. A	14. A	24. B	34. B
5. B	15. B	25. A	35. C
6. D	16. C	26. D	36. C
7. C	17. C	27. D	37. D
8. D	18. C	28. D	38. B
9. B	19. C	29. B	39. C
10. D	20. B	30. D	40. A

TEST 2

DIRECTIONS: Each question or incomplete statement is followed by several suggested answers or completions. Select the one that BEST answers the question or completes the statement. *PRINT THE LETTER OF THE CORRECT ANSWER IN THE SPACE AT THE RIGHT.*

1. A flagman, who is in front of a work crew on the roadway, signals a train to stop. After the work crew clears the roadway, the flagman gives the motorman a go-ahead signal using the wrong color lamp.
   The PROPER action for the motorman is to

   A. question the flagman giving the signal before moving the train ahead
   B. contact the desk trainmaster before moving the train ahead
   C. assume the signal is correct and proceed very slowly, prepared to stop within range of vision
   D. assume the signal may not be correct and proceed very slowly, prepared to stop within range of vision

   1.____

2. When disconnecting a third rail emergency jumper, it is IMPORTANT to

   A. remove the jumper end on the third rail first
   B. remove the jumper end on the car contact shoe first
   C. first place the master controller in the switching position
   D. remove both ends of the jumper at the same time

   2.____

3. The MOST important reason for requiring an employee to make out an accident report as soon as possible after an accident is to

   A. show that he is fit for duty
   B. discover conditions that cause accidents so that these conditions can be corrected
   C. make sure that no one forgets to file the report
   D. make sure that the person responsible for the accident is disciplined

   3.____

4. When a train is at a terminal and the motorman's indication is NOT working, this train can

   A. not leave carrying passengers
   B. leave carrying passengers if authorized by the train dispatcher
   C. leave carrying passengers, provided the conductor's indication is working for each side of the train
   D. leave carrying passengers, provided two conductors are stationed on the train to operate the doors

   4.____

5. A repeater signal would MOST likely be used

   A. at a terminal   B. on a curve
   C. in a yard   D. in a tower

   5.____

6. Water should NOT be used to put out electrical fires or fires that are near energized electrical equipment MAINLY because the water may

   A. cause harmful vapors   B. transmit a shock
   C. spread the fire   D. damage equipment

   6.____

7. The MOST probable cause of most accidents is

   A. inferior equipment
   B. lack of safety devices
   C. poor safety rules
   D. carelessness

8. When an absolute block has been set up on a section of the roadway, MOST likely there would be

   A. no trains running in this section due to an accident
   B. only work trains running in one direction in this section
   C. faulty signaling in this section
   D. single track operation in this section

9. When a motorman sees a stop arm hooked down, he is required to

   A. proceed with extreme caution and to pass the signal at a restricted speed
   B. stop and stay for 3 minutes before calling the desk trainmaster
   C. immediately report the location and signal number to the desk trainmaster
   D. signal for a signal maintainer using the train horn or whistle

10. An emergency alarm location, which is indicated by a blue light, has the following equipment: An emergency alarm

    A. only
    B. and a telephone only
    C. a telephone, and a fire extinguisher
    D. a telephone, a fire extinguisher, and a first aid kit

11. When coupling cars together, a motorman must make several stops at a certain distance each from the standing car. In bad weather, the FIRST stop should be at least

    A. 2 car lengths away
    B. 3 car lengths away
    C. 4 car lengths away
    D. twice the distance as in good weather

12. When a motorman is moving into a shop, he

    A. must blow the train whistle or horn three times
    B. must make sure the shop door is open high enough to pass through
    C. is permitted to move at a speed of 10 mph
    D. must bring the train to a stop just inside the shop door before proceeding

13. When coupling trains on a grade,

    A. the smaller number of cars must be coupled to the larger
    B. the larger number of cars must be coupled to the smaller
    C. all movements must be made downgrade
    D. all movements must be made upgrade

14. A train may run on flooded tracks provided the desk trainmaster has given permission and provided the water is below a certain level.
    This level is the

- A. top of the ties
- B. bottom flange of the running rail
- C. base of the running rail
- D. ball of the running rail

15. If the third rail power should go off while a local train is moving enroute between stations, the motorman should

    - A. allow the train to coast to the next station enroute or to an emergency exit between stations, if possible
    - B. allow the train to coast to the next interlocking tower location, if possible
    - C. allow the train to coast to an emergency alarm or to an emergency exit location, if possible
    - D. stop the train immediately and contact the desk trainmaster by radio or telephone

16. Before moving a train from a yard or lay-up track, a motorman must perform a rolling test. The purpose of this test is to check that the

    - A. electro-pneumatic brakes can stop the train
    - B. electro-pneumatic brakes release properly
    - C. dynamic brake is operating properly
    - D. hand brakes are operating properly

17. A 10 car passenger train is enroute and, because of an emergency situation, it becomes necessary to cut out the brakes on certain cars.
    Provided the train has enough braking power to safely carry passengers, this train may continue in passenger service if the brakes have been cut out on NO more than _____ an end car.

    - A. one car, which can also be
    - B. two cars, either of which can be
    - C. three cars, one of which is
    - D. four cars, none of which is

18. Hand brakes must NOT be released on a train until

    - A. a standing brake test has been made
    - B. the emergency brake valve has been released and the motorman is prepared to make a rolling test
    - C. the air brake system has been fully charged and the brakes are fully released
    - D. the air brake system has been fully charged and the brakes applied in emergency

19. When a train is enroute and it becomes necessary to cut out the brakes on either the head car or the rear car, it is then necessary to have an employee on the car with the cut out brakes in order to

    - A. apply the hand brake in case that car should uncouple from the train
    - B. signal the motorman when he may start the train at the remaining stations of that line
    - C. make sure that passengers do not enter that car at the remaining stations of that line
    - D. pull the emergency brake on that car if it becomes necessary to do so

20. Unless otherwise ordered or unless a diverging route sign shows another speed, the maximum speed at which a train may travel when moving to the left or right over a switch is _____ mph.

    A. 5   B. 10   C. 15   D. 20

21. When applying hand brakes on a train which is on level tracks, the hand brakes must be applied on

    A. the upgrade end of the train
    B. the end of the train that will be the front end when the train is next moved
    C. both ends of the train
    D. at least 1/3 of the cars of the train

22. If a train runs by a red stop signal, it is LEAST likely that there will be

    A. a delay in train service
    B. damage to the train
    C. injury to passengers
    D. damage to the automatic stop

23. The MAXIMUM speed for operating a single car is

    A. 10 mph and the controller must not be advanced beyond the series position
    B. 15 mph and the controller must not be advanced beyond the series position
    C. 20 mph and the controller must not be advanced beyond the series position
    D. the same as the maximum speed for a train consisting of several cars when conditions are normal

24. In a river tunnel, a train may NOT go faster than _____ mph.

    A. 20   B. 25   C. 30   D. 35

25. A motorman moving cars or trains in a yard or on storage tracks must NOT move faster than _____ mph.

    A. 5   B. 10   C. 15   D. 20

26. When it becomes necessary for the motorman of an enroute passenger train to use the train-to-wayside radio system and to identify his train, he should identify his train by stating

    A. the number of the leading car
    B. his name and the present location of the train
    C. the name of the leaving terminal and the schedule time of departure
    D. the name of the leaving terminal and the present location of the train

27. A diamond crossover has _____ turnout(s).

    A. no   B. 1   C. 2   D. 4

28. When a motorman sees an automatic signal that is unlit, he should

    A. immediately stop and signal for a signal maintainer
    B. pass the signal at restricted speed with extreme caution

C. immediately stop and notify the desk trainmaster
D. note the signal number and report it to the train dispatcher when he reaches the terminal

29. Track is classified as:
Type I - _____; Type II - _____; and Type III - _____.

   A. Structure; Ballast; Concrete
   B. Structure; Concrete; Ballast
   C. Ballast; Concrete; Structure
   D. Ballast; Structure; Concrete

30. A gap train is a(n)

   A. extra train held in reserve to take the place of a train that is taken out of service
   B. train that has been put in passenger service over and above the normal service requirements as provided by the train schedule
   C. train which stops at key stations and which is properly spaced
   D. train that has been abandoned or removed from service due to one or more reasons

31. Center excess is a term used to refer to the

   A. portion of a car body, at its center, which extends beyond the normal line of clearance on curved track
   B. amount of sway of a car body at its center
   C. gauge of track on curves
   D. super elevation, in inches, of the outside rail over the inside rail on curves

32. A work train may NOT leave a yard or terminal when there is fog unless permission has been obtained from the

   A. yardmaster   B. train dispatcher
   C. desk trainmaster   D. zone trainmaster

33. In order to restore third rail power in an area where the power was removed due to an emergency, it is necessary to call the desk trainmaster.
The employee who is responsible for contacting the trainmaster in order to restore the power is

   A. only the person who requested the power to be removed
   B. either the person who requested the power to be removed or a supervisor who assumed responsibility during the emergency
   C. only a supervisor
   D. either a member of the power department or the zone trainmaster

34. The highest ranking employee in the rapid transit operations department who is stationed at a terminal is USUALLY a(n)

   A. assistant train dispatcher
   B. train dispatcher
   C. assistant superintendent
   D. road car inspector

35. When a motorman has moved the ME-23 brake valve handle to its further position on the left, he has placed the handle in the _____ position.

    A. release
    B. emergency
    C. electric holding
    D. lap

36. Before a motorman couples cars together, he must make sure that the couplers to be joined are aligned and that their electric portion slides are fully _____ and their shutters are _____.

    A. retrieved; closed
    B. retrieved; open
    C. extended; closed
    D. extended; open

37. A car equipped with an H2C coupler and a car equipped with an H2A coupler can

    A. not be coupled together
    B. be coupled together mechanically only
    C. be coupled together electrically only
    D. be coupled together mechanically and electrically

38. IRT transfer cars that are equipped with a diversion valve have _____ trip cocks.

    A. no
    B. only one
    C. two
    D. four

39. The brake equipment on R-I to R-9 cars is _____ type.

    A. SMEE
    B. straight air brake
    C. AMUE
    D. H2A

40. The doors of R-10 to R-42 cars are operated by means of

    A. electrical door operators only
    B. either pneumatic door engines or hydraulic door engines
    C. hydraulic door engines only
    D. either electrical door operators or pneumatic door engines

KEY (CORRECT ANSWERS)

1.	A	11.	B	21.	B	31.	A
2.	A	12.	B	22.	D	32.	C
3.	B	13.	D	23.	A	33.	B
4.	A	14.	D	24.	D	34.	B
5.	B	15.	A	25.	B	35.	A
6.	B	16.	B	26.	C	36.	A
7.	D	17.	C	27.	D	37.	B
8.	D	18.	D	28.	C	38.	D
9.	C	19.	A	29.	C	39.	C
10.	C	20.	B	30.	A	40.	D

EXAMINATION SECTION
TEST 1

DIRECTIONS: Each question or incomplete statement is followed by several suggested answers or completions. Select the one that BEST answers the question or completes the statement. *PRINT THE LETTER OF THE CORRECT ANSWER IN THE SPACE AT THE RIGHT.*

1. As used in the transit system, the term *work motors* applies to

    A. large motors used for pumping water from flooded parts of the roadway
    B. cars used to pull other cars that do not have their own motive power
    C. door engines
    D. fan motors

2. As used in the transit system, the term *collection train* applies to a

    A. train that is carrying passengers
    B. train that picks up money collected by railroad clerks
    C. train that picks up refuse
    D. work train

3. Train delays are MOST frequently caused by

    A. door engine malfunctions
    B. low third rail voltage
    C. excessive heat from car heaters
    D. poor tractive power

4. Motormen are required to report all car failures on the

    A. Car Trips report
    B. Train Register sheet
    C. Record of Crew sheet
    D. Car Defect sheet

5. A contact shoe slipper is USUALLY found in a motorman's cab, and it is used

    A. as a replacement for a contact shoe
    B. to lubricate contact shoes
    C. to electrically insulate a contact shoe from the third rail
    D. to charge the batteries in a car

6. If one shoe of a subway car is touching the third rail, the number of shoes alive with electricity on that car is

    A. 1   B. 2   C. 3   D. 4

7. The normal voltage of the third rail in the subway is NEAREST to _____ volts.

    A. 300   B. 400   C. 500   D. 600

8. The storage battery on subway cars has an average voltage NEAREST to _____ volts.

    A. 15   B. 35   C. 55   D. 65

9. In order to operate a train consisting of R-10 type cars at its fastest speed, the master controller MUST be in the _____ position.

   A. multiple   B. series   C. switching   D. center

10. The MAIN reason for not operating a train for a long period of time in the switching position is to avoid

   A. slow speed operation
   B. excessive current flow through contact shoes
   C. waste of power
   D. probable damage to the car equipment

11. SMEE type brakes are

   A. electric   B. pneumatic
   C. electro-pneumatic   D. mechanical

12. The reverser key of R-10 type car equipment has three positions. These positions are

   A. first reverse, second reverse, third reverse
   B. forward, center, and off
   C. forward, center, and reverse
   D. first, second, and third

13. On R-10 type car equipment, the reverser key controls the direction of rotation of the

   A. fan motors   B. traction motors
   C. door engines   D. M3A feed valve

14. On cars equipped with SMEE type brakes, the red needle of the duplex air gauge indicates _____ pressure.

   A. straight air pipe   B. brake pipe
   C. main reservoir   D. compressor

15. On cars equipped with SMEE type brakes, the black needle of the duplex air gauge indicates _____ pressure.

   A. straight air pipe   B. brake pipe
   C. main reservoir   D. compressor

16. Angle cocks GENERALLY are used in a train's _____ system.

   A. propulsion   B. lighting
   C. braking   D. buzzer

17. R-10 type cars are equipped with

   A. ME-42 brake valves   B. ME-23 brake valves
   C. J1 couplers   D. UE5 universal valves

18. To charge the brake pipe on R-10 type car equipment, the motorman should place the brake valve in the _____ position.

   A. full service   B. handle up
   C. release   D. lap

19. On a particular subway line, the station platforms are 600 feet in length. The MAXIMUM number of proposed new 75-foot long cars that a train on this line can have is _____ cars.

   A. 4   B. 6   C. 8   D. 10

20. The train whistle or train horn signal that means *train has run by or stopped short of station platform* is

   A. 3 short blasts
   B. 1 long blast
   C. 1 long blast, 1 short blast
   D. 2 long blasts, 2 short blasts

21. The train whistle or train horn signal that means *signal maintainer respond to train* is

   A. 3 short blasts
   B. 1 long blast
   C. 1 long blast, 1 short blast
   D. 2 long blasts, 2 short blasts

22. The train whistle or train horn signal that means *train needs road car inspector* is

   A. 3 short blasts
   B. 1 long blast
   C. 1 long blast, 1 short blast
   D. 2 long blasts, 2 short blasts

23. The route request telephone located at a home signal is connected DIRECTLY to the

   A. yardmaster's office
   B. local tower
   C. central control desk
   D. chief train dispatcher's office

24. In locations where there is no alarm box, power to the third rail can be cut off by calling

   A. a road car inspector
   B. the terminal dispatcher
   C. the local interlocking tower
   D. the desk trainmaster

25. When calling for an ambulance, the MOST important information for the motorman to give is

   A. the nature of the injuries
   B. the location where the ambulance is required
   C. his name and pass number
   D. the probable cause of the accident

26. A motorman's weekly pay for 8 hours a day, 5 days a week, at $13.50 an hour is

   A. $108.00   B. $480.00   C. $540.00   D. $555.00

27. The buzzer signal that indicates to the motorman to PROCEED is _____ buzz(es).

    A. one short   B. two short
    C. one long   D. two long

28. The buzzer signal that indicates to the motorman to STOP is _____ buzz(es).

    A. one short   B. two short
    C. one long   D. two long

Questions 29-40.

DIRECTIONS: Questions 29 through 40 are based on the figures shown below of color light signals and signs used on the transit system. In figures 1 to 10 only, G means green lens is lighted, Y means yellow lens is lighted, R means red lens is lighted, and an S means that an S signal is lighted.

29. The signal that indicates proceed on diverging route is shown in figure

    A. 1   B. 3   C. 4   D. 7

30. The signal that indicates proceed on diverging route prepared to stop at next signal is shown in figure

    A. 3   B. 4   C. 8   D. 9

31. The signal that indicates stop and stay is shown in figure   31._____

    A. 2   B. 4   C. 6   D. 10

32. The signal shown in figure 9 indicates   32._____

    A. stop and key-by
    B. stop and call station office
    C. approach at allowable speed
    D. proceed

33. The signal that indicates proceed on main route is shown in figure   33._____

    A. 1   B. 2   C. 5   D. 8

34. The signal that indicates proceed on main route prepared to stop at next signal is shown in figure   34._____

    A. 2   B. 5   C. 8   D. 9

35. The signal that indicates proceed prepared to stop at next signal is shown in figure   35._____

    A. 3   B. 6   C. 8   D. 10

36. The sign that indicates resume speed is shown in figure   36._____

    A. 13   B. 14   C. 15   D. 16

37. The sign that indicates that block signaling stops at this point is shown in figure   37._____

    A. 11   B. 12   C. 13   D. 14

38. The sign shown in figure 11 indicates   38._____

    A. an emergency telephone location
    B. the location of an employee loading platform
    C. the location of route request buttons
    D. the beginning of time control

39. The sign shown in figure 12 is used to indicate the allowable speed   39._____

    A. for a downgrade
    B. for a diverging route
    C. when approaching a dead end
    D. in a danger zone

40. The sign shown in figure 15 is a _____ sign.   40._____

    A. gap filler
    B. resume speed
    C. reverse movement car stop
    D. station car stop

KEY (CORRECT ANSWERS)

1. B	11. C	21. C	31. C
2. B	12. C	22. A	32. C
3. A	13. B	23. B	33. A
4. D	14. A	24. D	34. B
5. C	15. B	25. B	35. C
6. D	16. C	26. C	36. A
7. D	17. A	27. D	37. D
8. B	18. A	28. C	38. D
9. A	19. C	29. B	39. B
10. D	20. D	30. B	40. D

TEST 2

DIRECTIONS: Each question or incomplete statement is followed by several suggested answers or completions. Select the one that BEST answers the question or completes the statement. *PRINT THE LETTER OF THE CORRECT ANSWER IN THE SPACE AT THE RIGHT.*

1. According to the rules, when operating trains in a yard, motormen must NOT advance their controllers beyond the _____ position. 1.____

   A. release   B. multiple   C. switching   D. series

2. If a scheduled maximum-length passenger train during non-rush hours is carrying about 50% more than the normal load for its trip, this is an indication that MOST likely 2.____

   A. a train ahead has been taken out of service
   B. its leader is running behind schedule
   C. this train is running one car short
   D. this train is running ahead of schedule

3. According to the rules, unless otherwise ordered or designated by a Diverging Route sign, the speed of trains over diverging routes is RESTRICTED to _____ M.P.H. 3.____

   A. 10   B. 15   C. 20   D. 25

4. According to the rules, motormen must stop their trains a certain minimum distance from a flagman's red flags or red lamps. This MINIMUM distance is _____ car length(s). 4.____

   A. one-half   B. one   C. two   D. three

5. A safety precaution to be taken by a motorman who is keying-by an automatic signal is to 5.____

   A. make sure stop arm is down
   B. wait for call-on before proceeding
   C. wait for a road car inspector
   D. sound train whistle as he passes signal

6. At any time when a motorman's vision is limited by rain, snow or fog, he MUST run his train 6.____

   A. to meet the schedule time
   B. at maximum speed
   C. without regard to these conditions
   D. so that he can stop within range of vision

7. If the third rail power should go off while a local train is enroute between two stations, the BEST action for the motorman to take is to 7.____

   A. blow whistle several times and make a light brake application
   B. make an immediate train stop
   C. use by-pass button to supply emergency battery power to traction motors
   D. attempt to coast to the next station

8. According to the rules, a motorman who is operating a work train that is skipping stations must

   A. receive permission from trainmaster to skip stations
   B. not sound the train whistle when passing through a subway station
   C. not exceed 15 M.P.H. when passing any station platform
   D. stop the train when approaching each station

9. The POOREST practice to be followed by a motorman when using the train radio is to

   A. decide what to say before transmitting
   B. speak very fast so as to reduce time on the air
   C. depress the transmitter switch when transmitting
   D. give his location when transmitting

10. The PRIMARY reason for requiring motormen, when they report for duty, to examine the bulletin board is to

    A. have train dispatcher observe their condition
    B. keep them busy until their first trip
    C. acquaint them with new rules
    D. make sure they know the conductor assigned to the run

11. Train crews are required to be familiar with the scheduled running time and arrival time at gap points and terminals for their run assignments.
    The MOST logical reason for this requirement is

    A. that both members of the crew are responsible for having the train at check points on time
    B. that crews should be able to answer passengers' questions
    C. for the crews to be aware of any overtime due to late arrival at the terminal
    D. so the crews can be checked for on-time performance

12. The employee in charge of train operations in a yard is USUALLY a

    A. yardmaster   B. train dispatcher
    C. motorman instructor D. towerman

13. The employee responsible for signal operations at an interlocking is USUALLY a(n)

    A. assistant train dispatcher
    B. train dispatcher
    C. towerman
    D. schedule maker

14. Emergency third rail jumpers are provided at certain locations on the transit system. These jumpers are USUALLY used to provide

    A. additional power for station lighting
    B. a reserve power supply for interlocking towers
    C. additional power for air conditioned subway cars
    D. power to a train stalled at a third rail gap

15. It is MOST important for the motorman to know the number of cars in his train so that he can   15._____

    A. make proper station stops
    B. judge the power to be applied to the train
    C. make sure the brake pipe pressure is correct
    D. judge the running time between stations

16. A seven-track layup yard can hold 16 cars on each track, but there are already five 8-car trains in this yard. The number of ADDITIONAL cars that can be stored in this yard is   16._____

    A. 40   B. 60   C. 72   D. 112

17. According to the rules, a motorman at a terminal should be at his operating position   17._____

    A. at least one interval ahead of time
    B. when the conductor says train is ready for service
    C. at least two minutes before scheduled leaving time
    D. as soon as his train is scheduled to leave

18. According to the rules, a motorman   18._____

    A. should coast as little as possible consistent with the schedule
    B. must back up a train if he has overrun the station platform
    C. must run as quickly as possible between stations in order to reduce headway
    D. should accept an alternate route if it does not take him off his scheduled line

19. When laying up a train on a grade, a motorman must apply sufficient hand brakes on the   19._____

    A. upgrade end of the train
    B. downgrade end of the train
    C. end closest to the terminal
    D. end which is to be the leaving end

20. In an emergency, when a motorman is authorized to make a reverse direction movement, he should   20._____

    A. operate with extreme caution
    B. back the train up at 10 M.P.H.
    C. operate at normal speed
    D. back the train up quickly

21. If a train takes 4 minutes to travel between 2 stations that are 1 mile apart, the average speed of the train is APPROXIMATELY _____ M.P.H.   21._____

    A. 5   B. 15   C. 25   D. 35

22. When a motorman is forced to operate a train from a position other than the leading car, he must NOT move the master controller handle beyond the _____ position.   22._____

    A. switching   B. release   C. multiple   D. series

23. When the stop arm of a signal has been *hooked down*, it means that the stop arm   23._____

    A. has been removed for repair
    B. is not in position to trip the brakes of a train

C. is in position to trip the brakes of a train
D. is not in the clear position

24. A portable train stop would MOST likely be used by a
    A. towerman   B. train dispatcher
    C. conductor   D. flagman

25. Dwarf signals are
    A. used for high speed train movements
    B. located in an interlocking tower
    C. not used in the transit system
    D. low home signals

26. In a two-hour period, eight trains pass a gap station. The average headway between trains is CLOSEST to _____ minutes.
    A. 9   B. 12   C. 15   D. 22

27. A no clearance area in the transit system is indicated by a sign that
    A. has red and white diagonal stripes
    B. has black and white diagonal stripes
    C. is all red
    D. is all white

28. The MOST serious result of a motorman running a train past a red signal is
    A. damage to wayside equipment
    B. injury to passengers
    C. delay to train service
    D. damage to the automatic stop

29. A blue light located along the subway trackway indicates a(n)
    A. interlocking tower   B. home signal
    C. no clearance area   D. emergency alarm location

30. A switch target is a fixed signal GENERALLY associated with a
    A. route request button
    B. time control sign
    C. gap filler signal
    D. hand-operated switch in a yard

31. A train dispatcher at a gap point USUALLY controls the starting or holding of a train at the gap station by means of
    A. a train order signal
    B. groups of three amber lights on the platform
    C. flag signals
    D. the platform's public address system

32. A motorman who is given a proceed signal with a yellow light by a flagman should expect to

    A. find the track ahead blocked by a disabled train
    B. encounter another flagman further up the track
    C. key-by the next automatic signal
    D. operate into a station against the normal traffic direction

33. When a motorman encounters any caution light or flags on the track, he must immediately reduce speed to NOT more than _____ M.P.H. and sound _____ whistle blast(s).

    A. 10; two long
    B. 15; repeated short
    C. 15; one long
    D. 10; one short

34. Due to a car equipment failure, it may become necessary for a motorman to operate a work train from other than the head end. In this case, a flagman must be stationed at the head end to continuously relay information to the motorman.
    If the motorman fails to receive continuous communication from the flagman by means of radio or sound-powered telephone, he MUST

    A. immediately use flashlight signals
    B. proceed slowly
    C. stop the train and investigate
    D. operate the master controller in the multiple position

35. A lighted motorman's indication informs the motorman that the

    A. side doors are closed and locked
    B. train headlights are on
    C. train battery is charged
    D. brake pipe pressure is below normal

36. A person can travel to Citi Field by subway. Citi Field is located in

    A. Manhattan
    B. Queens
    C. the Bronx
    D. Brooklyn

37. A person can travel to Lincoln Center by subway. Lincoln Center is located in

    A. Manhattan
    B. Queens
    C. the Bronx
    D. Brooklyn

38. There is NO rapid transit rail service which directly serves

    A. the Bronx Zoo
    B. Prospect Park
    C. LaGuardia Airport
    D. the Rockaways

39. A person can travel to the New York Aquarium by subway. The New York Aquarium is located in

    A. Manhattan
    B. Queens
    C. the Bronx
    D. Brooklyn

40. South Street Seaport is
    A. in Coney Island
    B. on the East River near the Brooklyn Bridge
    C. near LaGuardia Airport
    D. in St. George on Staten Island

40.____

KEY (CORRECT ANSWERS)

1. D	11. A	21. B	31. B
2. A	12. A	22. D	32. B
3. A	13. C	23. B	33. A
4. B	14. D	24. D	34. C
5. A	15. A	25. D	35. A
6. D	16. C	26. C	36. B
7. D	17. C	27. A	37. A
8. C	18. D	28. B	38. C
9. B	19. B	29. D	39. D
10. C	20. A	30. D	40. B

EXAMINATION SECTION
TEST 1

DIRECTIONS: Each question or incomplete statement is followed by several suggested answers or completions. Select the one that BEST answers the question or completes the statement. *PRINT THE LETTER OF THE CORRECT ANSWER IN THE SPACE AT THE RIGHT.*

1. On married pair cars, motor generators are provided 1.____
   - A. instead of batteries
   - B. on each car
   - C. on even-numbered cars only
   - D. on odd-numbered cars only

2. The number of traction motors in each car is 2.____
   - A. 1
   - B. 2
   - C. 4
   - D. 6

3. The device that electrically insulates the contact shoe from the truck is called the 3.____
   - A. contact shoe slipper
   - B. main knife switch
   - C. shoe beam
   - D. main motor fuse

4. The contact shoe is held on the third rail 4.____
   - A. electrically
   - B. pneumatically
   - C. by a magnet
   - D. by a spring

5. The power source that furnishes energy for the heaters and fans on cars has a voltage of 5.____
   - A. 120 volts AC
   - B. 600 volts AC
   - C. 120 volts DC
   - D. 600 volts DC

6. When a motorman opens a live main knife switch, he must do it with 6.____
   - A. a rapid motion
   - B. the main resistor coil disconnected
   - C. the 600-volt cab panel board switches in a closed position
   - D. the main motor fuse removed

7. A blown B2 circuit breaker affects the operation of the 7.____
   - A. doors
   - B. brakes
   - C. guard lights
   - D. motorman's indication light

8. The straight air pipe angle cock should be painted 8.____
   - A. red
   - B. green
   - C. yellow
   - D. black

9. When the straight air pipe angle cock is closed, its handle is 9.____
   - A. turned to the left
   - B. turned to the right
   - C. "out" all the way
   - D. "in" all the way

10. When the ME-42 brake valve handle is in the farthest position on the left, it is in the "full release" position. The *next* position to the right is the 10.____
    - A. "handle off" position
    - B. "running release" position
    - C. "emergency" position
    - D. "full service" position

37

11. There are five positions for the ME-42 brake valve. The middle position is the

    A. "handle off" position
    B. "lap" position
    C. "emergency" position
    D. "full service" position

12. On brake valve-type equipment, the brake valve handle can be removed when it is in the

    A. "handle off" position
    B. "running release" position
    C. "full release" position
    D. "electric holding" position

13. The duplex air gage needle that Indicates brake pipe pressure is colored

    A. red   B. yellow   C. black   D. amber

14. There are no brakes applied when the brake valve handle is in the

    A. "full service" position
    B. "full release" position
    C. "handle off" position
    D. "electric holding" position

15. When the brake valve handle is in the "full release" position, the straight air pipe pressure should be

    A. 0 psi   B. 50 psi   C. 72 psi   D. 110 psi

16. When the master controller is in the farthese position to the right, it is in the "off" position. The *next* position to the left is the

    A. "multiple" position
    B. "series" position
    C. "center" position
    D. "switching" position

17. When a train is in operation, all the master controller reverser drums except the one in the motorman's operating cab should be in the

    A. "center" position
    B. "forward" position
    C. "reverse" position
    D. "multiple" position

18. The master controller is provided with a by-pass button so that it can operate even though

    A. its battery has run down
    B. the door relay is open
    C. a traction motor has a short
    D. the "dead man's" feature is broken

19. When a motorman is coupling together two parts of a train that are ten feet apart, it is BEST for him to put the master controller in the

    A. "multiple" position
    B. "series" position
    C. "center" position
    D. "switching" position

20. When approximately one-half the maximum speed of a train is desired, the master controller should be put in the

  A. "multiple" position   B. "parallel" position
  C. "series" position   D. "switching" position

20.____

KEY (CORRECT ANSWERS)

1.	C	11.	D
2.	C	12.	A
3.	C	13.	C
4.	D	14.	B
5.	D	15.	A
6.	A	16.	D
7.	B	17.	A
8.	A	18.	B
9.	C	19.	D
10.	B	20.	C

TEST 2

DIRECTIONS: Each question or incomplete statement is followed by several suggested answers or completions. Select the one that BEST answers the question or completes the statement. *PRINT THE LETTER OF THE CORRECT ANSWER IN THE SPACE AT THE RIGHT.*

1. The tower horn signal consisting of one long blast means that   1.____

   A. all the trains in the interlocking limits may proceed
   B. all the trains in the interlocking limits must come to an immediate stop
   C. the train has run past or stopped short of the station platform
   D. the road car inspector should contact the tower

2. The tower horn signal at an interlocking consisting of two short blasts means that the   2.____

   A. signal maintainer should contact the tower
   B. trains in the interlocking limits must come to an immediate stop
   C. road car inspector should contact the tower
   D. trains in the interlocking limits may proceed

3. The train horn signal consisting of two long blasts   3.____

   A. is sounded when passing caution lights
   B. means that the train is requesting a route from the towerman
   C. means that the train needs a signal maintainer
   D. is an alarm to persons on or near the track

4. The train horn signal consisting of three short blasts means that the train   4.____

   A. has run past the station platform
   B. needs a road car inspector
   C. crew needs police assistance
   D. is requesting a route from the towerman

5. The train horn signal consisting of two short blasts   5.____

   A. means that the train has run past the station platform
   B. means that the train needs a signal maintainer
   C. is an alarm to persons on or near the track
   D. is an answer to any signal

6. The train buzzer signal consisting of two long buzzes and two short buzzes means that the   6.____

   A. motorman should sound the horn for the road car inspector
   B. train is making an irregular movement through the station
   C. train has run by or stopped short of the station platform
   D. motorman should sound the train horn for assistance

7. Cars that are used to provide motive power for pulling inoperative cars are called   7.____

   A. "drags"   B. "leaders'
   C. "pick-up cars"   D. "work motors"

8. On a gap sheet or train register sheet, the term "ABD" means a

   A. dropped interval
   B. flexible schedule
   C. revenue train
   D. collection train

9. After a motorman operates an emergency alarm box, he must use the telephone alongside the box to call the

   A. command center
   B. fire department
   C. police department
   D. power department

10. The signal aspect which requires a slow train speed movement past the signal into the yard is

    A. red over lunar white
    B. red over red over yellow
    C. yellow over yellow over yellow
    D. green over green

11. A signal that displays either two horizontal red lights or two horizontal lunar white lights is called a

    A. marker signal
    B. gap filler signal
    C. train order signal
    D. train holding signal

12. When the gap fillers are sufficiently withdrawn to clear the sides of the cars, the gap filler signal displays a(n)

    A. yellow over yellow over yellow aspect
    B. red over red over yellow aspect
    C. illuminated sign bearing the letters "GF" together with a green aspect
    D. illuminated sign bearing the letters "GF" and the track designation

13. The signal aspect which means *proceed on the main route* is

    A. yellow over yellow
    B. green over green
    C. yellow
    D. lunar white

14. The signal aspect which means *proceed on the main route and be prepared to stop at the next signal* is

    A. yellow over green
    B. green over yellow
    C. yellow over yellow
    D. red over lunar white

15. The signal aspect which means *approach at the allowable speed and then proceed on the diverging route* is

    A. red over red over yellow
    B. yellow over yellow with an illuminated S signal
    C. red over red with an illuminated D signal
    D. yellow over yellow over yellow

16. A starting signal for a train at a terminal has three _____ lights.

    A. green   B. amber   C. lunar white   D. blue

17. The signal aspect for a "call-on" is

    A. red over red over yellow
    B. yellow over yellow over yellow
    C. red over red over green
    D. yellow over yellow over green

18. A station time signal is used at certain locations to permit a train to

    A. leave a gap station even though it is ahead of schedule
    B. close in on a preceding train standing in a station
    C. leave a station even though the next signal aspect is red
    D. skip a station during certain hours of the day

19. An extra train that is held in reserve to take the place of a train that has been taken out of service for any reason is called a

    A. "pick-up train"   B. "follower"
    C. "drag"   D. "gap train"

20. A signal that NEVER has an automatic stop is a(n)

    A. approach signal   B. home signal
    C. automatic signal   D. repeater signal

KEY (CORRECT ANSWERS)

1.	B	11.	C
2.	D	12.	D
3.	A	13.	B
4.	B	14.	A
5.	D	15.	B
6.	C	16.	B
7.	D	17.	A
8.	A	18.	B
9.	A	19.	D
10.	C	20.	D

EXAMINATION SECTION
TEST 1

DIRECTIONS: Each question or incomplete statement is followed by several suggested answers or completions. Select the one that BEST answers the question or completes the statement. *PRINT THE LETTER OF THE CORRECT ANSWER IN THE SPACE AT THE RIGHT.*

1. The sign shown on the right is a
   A. reverse movement car stop sign
   B. station car stop sign
   C. resume speed sign
   D. reduce speed sign

2. A sign associated with an employee loading platform has the letter _____ on a white background
   A. "P"   B. "E"   C. "L"   D. "T"

3. A "no clearance area" is indicated by a sign that has _____ diagonal stripes.
   A. red and green
   B. red and black
   C. red and white
   D. black and white

4. The sign that indicates that the master controller of a train must not be advanced beyond the series position until the train reaches a "resume speed sign" has the letters
   A. ST   B. GT   C. SLOW   D. SERIES

5. The sign shown on the right indicates to a motorman of a train of 10 car-lengths to
   A. stop at this location for a movement in the opposite direction
   B. stop at this location when making a scheduled station stop
   C. resume speed when reaching this location
   D. reduce speed when reaching this location

6. A blue light along the right-of-way indicates the location of a(n)
   A. emergency exit
   B. tower
   C. emergency alarm box
   D. interlocking

7. The time interval between trains is called
   A. "schedule"   B. "headway"   C. "stretch"   D. "timetable"

8. A "housetop" is used at a
   A. switch point
   B. frog
   C. end incline
   D. curve

9. The type of track that has wooden ties bedded in ballast is type
   A. I   B. II   C. III   D. VIII

10. Of the following, the information *most likely* to be found on a bulletin board is

    A. "train schedules"
    B. "train trouble sheets"
    C. "general orders"
    D. "train register sheets"

11. The *MOST* important information for a motorman to give when calling for an ambulance for an injured passenger is

    A. the probable cause of the injuries
    B. where the ambulance is needed
    C. the injured man's name
    D. the motorman's name and pass number

12. The device used to electrically insulate a subway car from the third rail is called a(n)

    A. fibre tie pad
    B. frog
    C. insulated joint
    D. contact shoe slipper

13. The power source that furnishes energy for the "train to wayside" radio has a voltage of

    A. 60 volts AC
    B. 600 volts AC
    C. 32 volts DC
    D. 600 volts DC

14. When running a train from other than the front end, communication between the flagman in the front cab and the motorman must be made by means of

    A. the train buzzer signals
    B. the train public address system
    C. sound-powered telephone
    D. hand signals

15. When uncoupling passenger cars, the *first* item to disconnect is the

    A. electrical connection
    B. pneumatic connection
    C. mechanical connection
    D. chains between the cars

16. When a flagman motions with the wrong color lamp to a motorman to proceed, the motorman should

    A. call the command center
    B. question the flagman
    C. first stop and then proceed with caution
    D. proceed at the normal speed

17. When a motorman's indication fails to work at a terminal, the train can leave carrying passengers *only if*

    A. the train has more than one conductor
    B. a sound powered telephone is available
    C. the conductor's indication is working properly
    D. the trouble has been corrected

18. When a train is coming into a terminal track that ends in a bumper block, it must *NOT* go faster than

    A. 3 mph   B. 5 mph   C. 7 mph   D. 10 mph

19. When an 8-car train is stopped in an area where power has been shut off for 30 minutes or more, handbrakes must be applied on _____ of the cars of the train.

    A. at least 1/4
    B. at least 1/3
    C. at least 1/2
    D. all

20. Of the following, train delays are MOST frequently caused by

    A. low third-rail voltage
    B. poor tractive power
    C. door trouble
    D. trains being tripped

KEY (CORRECT ANSWERS)

1.	B	11.	B
2.	A	12.	D
3.	C	13.	C
4.	D	14.	C
5.	A	15.	D
6.	C	16.	B
7.	B	17.	D
8.	A	18.	D
9.	A	19.	C
10.	C	20.	C

TEST 2

DIRECTIONS: Each question or incomplete statement is followed by several suggested answers or completions. Select the one that BEST answers the question or completes the statement. *PRINT THE LETTER OF THE CORRECT ANSWER IN THE SPACE AT THE RIGHT.*

1. If a motorman's indication fails to work after the train has left the terminal, the

   A. train should continue to carry passengers, but the conductor must use the buzzer
   B. passengers must be removed from the train at the next station
   C. train should continue with passengers if there are two conductors present
   D. train must not continue until a motorman instructor is present

1.___

2. When a train is traveling over a switch, the MAXIMUM speed allowed unless otherwise specified is

   A. 5 mph   B. 10 mph   C. 15 mph   D. 20 mph

2.___

3. In a river tunnel, a train should NOT go faster than

   A. 15 mph   B. 25 mph   C. 35 mph   D. 45 mph

3.___

4. If a certain motorman earns $708.00 each week and works 40 hours each week, his rate of pay per hour is

   A. $17.25   B. $17.40   C. $17.55   D. $17.70

4.___

5. A train moving at the rate of 30 miles per hour will travel 6 miles in

   A. 5 minutes   B. 8 minutes   C. 10 minutes   D. 12 minutes

5.___

6. When sound-powered telephones are used, it is important to establish positive communication by

   A. speaking in a convincing voice
   B. constant voice communication
   C. giving orders when you are sure of the situation
   D. responding immediately to orders

6.___

7. Motormen are usually NOT under the orders of a

   A. train dispatcher   B. trainmaster
   C. conductor   D. station supervisor

7.___

8. A train carrying passengers is in the terminal. This train must be taken out of service if the air brakes have been cut out on _____ of the cars.

   A. at least 1/4   B. at least 1/3
   C. at least 1/2   D. any

8.___

9. When coupling two trains with different types of air brakes, the trains must be coupled *only*

   A. electrically   B. mechanically
   C. electrically and mechanically   D. mechanically and pneumatically

9.___

46

10. The MAXIMUM speed allowed for a work train on straight track is

    A. 15 mph   B. 20 mph   C. 25 mph   D. 30 mph

11. The *main* reason for *NOT* operating a train for an extended period of time in the switching position is to

    A. prevent damage to the car equipment
    B. conserve power
    C. prevent accidents
    D. allow the train to operate automatically

12. The *LEAST* likely result of a train passing an automatic signal whose aspect is red is

    A. damage to the car equipment
    B. injuries to the passengers
    C. a delay in train service
    D. damage to the signal's automatic stop arm

13. All car equipment failures must be reported by the motorman

    A. to the road car inspector
    B. to the command center
    C. on the train register sheet
    D. on the car defect sheet

14. An employee who is *NOT* authorized to flag a train past a signal that is indicating stop is a

    A. towerman   B. train dispatcher
    C. station supervisor   D. signal maintainer

15. On the R-44 car, a door operator controls

    A. 1/2 of a double-door   B. 1 double-door
    C. 2 double-doors   D. 4 double-doors

16. Which of the following statements is correct about R-44 type equipment? The

    A. "A" car can be operated by a motorman without a "B" car
    B. "B" car can be operated by a motorman without an "A" car
    C. "A" car has two cabs
    D. "B" car has one cab

17. Inverters are used on R-42 cars to

    A. initiate the dynamic braking
    B. initiate the emergency braking
    C. change AC voltage to DC
    D. change DC voltage to AC

18. According to standard flagging instructions, the movement of a yellow light up and down is a signal to the motorman to
    A. proceed very slowly and to be prepared to stop within range of his vision
    B. proceed at a normal speed expecting the next light to be green
    C. proceed at a speed not to exceed 20 miles per hour
    D. stop and ask the flagman what the yellow light is for

19. According to standard flagging instructions, an *acceptable* distance for the yellow lamps to be placed ahead of the red lamp is
    A. 200 feet   B. 400 feet   C. 600 feet   D. 800 feet

20. If train speeds on a particular track are to be temporarily reduced to no more than ten miles per hour without the stationing of a flagman, the number of yellow lamps that should be placed on the track is
    A. 2   B. 3   C. 4   D. 5

KEY (CORRECT ANSWERS)

1.	A	11.	A
2.	B	12.	D
3.	C	13.	D
4.	D	14.	C
5.	D	15.	A
6.	B	16.	A
7.	D	17.	D
8.	D	18.	A
9.	B	19.	C
10.	C	20.	B

EXAMINATION SECTION
TEST 1

DIRECTIONS: Each question or incomplete statement is followed by several suggested answers or completions. Select the one that BEST answers the question or completes the statement. *PRINT THE LETTER OF THE CORRECT ANSWER IN THE SPACE AT THE RIGHT.*

1. The MAXIMUM speed of a train moving into a shop should be _____ miles per hour. 1._____

    A. 2 B. 5 C. 10 D. 15

2. A train is entering a terminal whose track ends in a bumping block. The MAXIMUM speed of the train as it enters the terminal should be _____ miles per hour. 2._____

    A. 3 B. 5 C. 7 D. 10

3. A Motorman notices that the stop arm of an automatic signal has failed to go down. The Motorman decides that he will hook the stop arm down and unhook it after he gets his train clear of the stop arm.
   Before he moves the stop arm, he must get permission from the 3._____

    A. Towerman
    C. Motorman Instructor
    B. Dispatcher
    D. Desk Trainmaster

4. Which of the following pieces of equipment of a train will NOT operate if the third rail power supply fails? 4._____

    A. Brakes
    C. Car body lights
    B. Motorman indication lights
    D. Air compressors

5. Call-on signals are displayed only on _____ signals. 5._____

    A. dwarf B. home C. automatic D. approach

6. As a Motorman pulls his train into a terminal, he gives three short blasts of his horn. The Motorman is requesting a 6._____

    A. Transit Patrolman
    C. Road Car Inspector
    B. Motorman Instructor
    D. Car Cleaner

7. The motor generators on trains made up of R-42 cars are ALWAYS located on 7._____

    A. each car
    C. the odd-numbered cars
    B. the even-numbered cars
    D. the front car *only*

8. How many traction motors are there on each passenger subway car? 8._____

    A. 1 B. 2 C. 4 D. 6

9. There are five positions on the ME-42 brake valve.
   The middle position is the _____ position. 9._____

    A. service range
    C. emergency
    B. handle-off
    D. lap

49

10. A blown B2 circuit breaker affects the operation of the

    A. guard lights
    B. brakes
    C. doors
    D. Motorman's indication light

11. When the straight air and brake pipe angle cocks are open, the position of the brake handles should be

    A. turned to the left   B. turned to the right
    C. all the way out   D. all the way in

12. Of the following, two long and two short buzzes from the Motorman to the Conductor tells the Conductor

    A. to sound the train horn for police assistance
    B. the train has stopped short of a station platform
    C. the train is making an irregular movement through the station
    D. to sound the train horn for the Road Car Inspector

13. After a Motorman operates an emergency alarm box, he should use the telephone alongside the box to call the

    A. Power Department   B. Police Department
    C. Fire Department   D. Command Center

14. A passenger train starts to move with an open door.
    What should be done with that train?
    It should be

    A. continued in service until it arrives at its terminal then be removed from service
    B. removed from service and sent to any yard
    C. removed from service and sent to the nearest yard with a barn or shop facility
    D. removed from service and placed on the nearest spur track

15. On SMEE equipment, the angle cocks which are painted yellow are ALWAYS located at

    A. the number 2 end of each married pair
    B. the number 1 end of each married pair
    C. both ends of each married pair
    D. both ends of the train rider car

16. The signal aspect for a *call-on* is

    A. yellow over yellow over red
    B. red over red over yellow
    C. yellow over yellow over yellow
    D. red over yellow over red

17. Which set of lights is a holding signal for the Motorman of a train in a gap station? _____ lights.

    A. Blue   B. Lunar white
    C. Amber   D. Green

18. The signal aspect that means proceed on the main route and be prepared to stop at the next signal is

    A. yellow over yellow
    B. green over yellow
    C. yellow over green
    D. red over lunar white

19. Which of the following is a signal that does NOT have an automatic stop? A(n) _____ signal.

    A. home
    B. approach
    C. automatic
    D. repeater

20. A sign with red and white diagonal stripes indicates a(n)

    A. *no clearance* area
    B. Conductor's indication board
    C. under-river tunnel emergency room
    D. temporary work project

21. The signal aspect that means proceed on the main route is

    A. yellow over green
    B. green over yellow
    C. green over green
    D. yellow over yellow

22. Before releasing any handbrakes on a train laid up on a grade, the Motorman is required to

    A. release the air brakes first
    B. place chocks under the wheels of the first car
    C. fully charge the air brake system and then apply the brakes in emergency
    D. apply the brakes in emergency and make sure there is third rail power

23. A Motorman contacts the Command Center about a 12-8 condition on his train. He is reporting a(n)

    A. disorderly passenger
    B. smoke condition on the train
    C. passenger under his train
    D. armed passenger

24. A Motorman calls the Command Center and reports a 12-2 condition on his train. Of the following, the Motorman is reporting a

    A. fire on his train
    B. derailment
    C. sick passenger
    D. serious case of vandalism

25. When the third rail jumper is to be used on an off-power train, the jumper should FIRST be applied to the

    A. contact shoe
    B. traction motors
    C. third rail
    D. main knife switch

26. The meaning of the radio code 12-5 is

    A. passenger on roadway
    B. vandalism
    C. stalled train
    D. a fight on the train

4 (#1)

27. What should the Motorman do if the power goes off while his passenger train is moving?

   A. Stop the train and call the Power Department.
   B. Stop and secure the train with handbrakes.
   C. Coast to the next station or nearest emergency exit.
   D. Stop and secure the train and discharge the passengers.

28. Which of the following signals in the B Division instructs the Motorman to proceed with caution on a diverging route?

   A. Yellow over red   B. Red over yellow
   C. Yellow over yellow   D. Green over yellow

29. Two horizontal red lights on a fixed signal inside a subway tunnel are known as a _____ signal.

   A. train holding   B. train identity
   C. repeater   D. train order

30. Which of the following signals in the B Division instructs the Motorman to proceed on a diverging route?

   A. Green over yellow   B. Yellow over green
   C. Yellow over yellow   D. Green over green

31. A signal with fixed red over red aspects on yard tracks instructing the Motorman to stop and stay is known as a(n) _____ signal.

   A. marker   B. home   C. bad order   D. automatic

32. Sudden stops on moving passenger trains should be avoided whenever possible MAINLY to avoid

   A. unnecessary delays
   B. excessive wear of the brakes
   C. injury to passengers
   D. train derailment

33. On a subway car, third rail power is used to operate which of the following? The

   A. Conductor's signal light
   B. Motorman's indication light
   C. tail lights
   D. car ventilating fans

34. A Motorman notices that the Towerman has set up the wrong route. The Motorman should blow on his horn _____ blast(s).

   A. one long   B. two short
   C. three short   D. four short

35. Single track operation is GENERALLY necessary under which of the following circumstances?

   A. A train with locked wheels blocks a main line.
   B. Running rails are being renewed in an express station.

C. Signal cables are being replaced in an under-river tunnel.
D. A train experiences a brake pipe rupture.

36. Which of the following two conditions must be met for a Motorman to operate his train on a flooded track?
The water level _____ the running rail and the _____ must give his permission.

   A. must be below the ball of; Motorman Instructor
   B. must be below the ball of; Desk Trainmaster
   C. may be up to the ball of; Superintendent
   D. may be slightly above; Desk Trainmaster

37. When approaching bumper blocks or other cars in the yard in good weather, a Motorman should FIRST make a complete stop of his train at a minimum distance of _____ car-length(s).

   A. 1   B. 2   C. 3   D. 4

38. For an 8-car train carrying passengers, what is the MINIMUM number of cars with air brakes cut out that would prohibit the Motorman from leaving the terminal?

   A. 1   B. 2   C. 4   D. 6

39. Operation of train with the controller in a switching position for an extended period is likely to result in

   A. burnt out switches
   B. wasteful use of power
   C. damage to the train cars' resistors
   D. excessive wear to the train cars' generator units

40. Which of the following is TRUE of an illuminated lunar white aspect?
It

   A. provides the Motorman with clearance before entering a station
   B. is associated with a stop indication
   C. instructs the Motorman to follow a diverging route
   D. instructs the Motorman to stop his train

KEY (CORRECT ANSWERS)

1.	B	11.	B	21.	D	31.	A
2.	C	12.	D	22.	B	32.	C
3.	C	13.	D	23.	A	33.	B
4.	B	14.	D	24.	A	34.	D
5.	C	15.	B	25.	D	35.	C
6.	B	16.	C	26.	C	36.	A
7.	B	17.	B	27.	A	37.	B
8.	D	18.	C	28.	B	38.	C
9.	C	19.	A	29.	B	39.	C
10.	B	20.	B	30.	B	40.	D

TEST 2

DIRECTIONS: Each question or incomplete statement is followed by several suggested answers or completions. Select the one that BEST answers the question or completes the statement. *PRINT THE LETTER OF THE CORRECT ANSWER IN THE SPACE AT THE RIGHT.*

1. When approaching bumper blocks or other cars in the yard in bad weather, a Motorman should make a complete stop of his train at a MINIMUM distance of _____ car length(s). 1._____

    A. 1   B. 2   C. 3   D. 4

2. When a repeated transmission by a Motorman to the Command Center is not answered, what should the Motorman do NEXT? 2._____
He should

    A. stop transmitting, continue to the terminal, and then report the problem to the Command Center
    B. continue to repeat the transmission, and give his location, car number, and nature of the problem
    C. assume that his transmission was received and cease transmitting to the Command Center
    D. stop another train, report the problem to the Motorman of that train, and ask that Motorman to relay the information to the Command Center

3. A Motorman is unable to reach the Command Center by radio to report a delay in service. 3._____
Upon arrival at a terminal, he should notify

    A. his Motorman Instructor
    B. the Division Superintendent
    C. the Command Center and the Dispatcher
    D. the Station Superintendent and the Dispatcher

4. A standard bank of 5 amber or yellow lights at the entrance of a slow-speed project area tells the Motorman that his MAXIMUM speed should be _____ miles per hour. 4._____

    A. 2   B. 5   C. 10   D. 15

5. When coupling subway cars, the smaller number of cars must be coupled to the larger number except 5._____

    A. at a terminal   B. on a grade
    C. at a bumping block   D. in a barn

6. Work trains may NOT leave a yard or terminal when there is a fog condition unless permission is granted by the 6._____

    A. Dispatcher   B. Motorman Instructor
    C. Desk Trainmaster   D. Towerman

7. The MAXIMUM speed of a work train operating on a storage track in a yard should be _____ miles per hour. 7._____

    A. 5   B. 10   C. 15   D. 25

8. The MAXIMUM speed of a train moving over a switch with no diverging sign should be _____ miles per hour.
   A. 5   B. 10   C. 15   D. 20

9. The MAXIMUM speed of a train in an under-river tube should be _____ miles per hour.
   A. 10   B. 15   C. 30   D. 35

10. Of the following, the LEAST important reason for removing a train from passenger service is a(n)
    A. open battery
    B. 8-inch flat wheel
    C. car lit by emergency lights only
    D. bad order (B.O.) brake valve in the operating car

11. The MAXIMUM speed of a train passing a station platform should be _____ miles per hour.
    A. 10   B. 15   C. 25   D. 30

12. The position of the brake valve handle on an ME-42 immediately to the left of its *handle off* position is the _____ position.
    A. running release   B. emergency
    C. full service   D. full release

13. The master controller is provided with a by-pass button in order for the Motorman to operate the train when
    A. a door relay is open
    B. a battery is run down
    C. there is a short in a traction motor
    D. the *dead man's feature* is energized

14. The brake valve handle can be removed from an ME-42 brake valve only if it is in the _____ position.
    A. handle off   B. full release
    C. emergency   D. full service

15. Brakes are NOT applied on a car when the brake valve handle is in the _____ position.
    A. emergency   B. handle off
    C. full service   D. running release

16. When the brake valve handle for the ME-42 brake valve is in the full service position, the straight air pipe pressure should be CLOSEST to _____ psi.
    A. 0   B. 52   C. 72   D. 112

17. On SMEE equipment, what color is the duplex air gauge needle that indicates straight air pipe pressure?
    A. Red   B. Black   C. Yellow   D. Green

18. The device that electrically insulates the truck from the contact shoe is the   18._____

    A. main motor fuse   B. wooden shoe beam
    C. wooden shoe slipper   D. main knife switch

19. Two short blasts of a train's horn mean that the Motorman is   19._____

    A. requesting a Car Inspector
    B. responding to a given signal
    C. alerting persons on or near the track
    D. requesting a Signal Maintainer

20. The Motorman takes orders from all of the following EXCEPT a   20._____

    A. Train Dispatcher   B. Station Supervisor
    C. Conductor   D. Trainmaster

21. Sound-powered phones are used on project work trains.   21._____
    Which of the following is the MOST important safety consideration when using these phones?

    A. Maintaining a constant voice communication
    B. Speaking in a loud voice
    C. Speaking at an even level of audibility
    D. Using standard railroad terms

22. On SMEE equipment, the supply pipe going from the odd-numbered car to the even-numbered car in a married pair leads the air into the _____ reservoir.   22._____

    A. main   B. auxiliary
    C. volume   D. supplementary

23. The sign to the right is a _____ sign.   23._____
    A. resume speed
    B. reduce speed
    C. station car stop
    D. reverse movement stop car

24. The sign to the right tells the Motorman operating a 10-car train to   24._____
    A. stop at the sign for a movement
    B. in the opposite direction B. stop at the sign when making a scheduled station stop
    C. resume speed when reaching the sign location
    D. reduce speed when reaching the sign location

25. A blue light along the subway right of way indicates the location of an   25._____

    A. emergency exit   B. emergency alarm box
    C. interlocking plant   D. emergency tower

26. If a Motorman's indication fails at a terminal, the train cannot leave with passengers unless   26._____

    A. sound-powered phones are used
    B. the Conductor's buzzer is working properly

C. a Road Car Inspector is aboard
D. the Motorman's indication has been restored

27. A train that has already left a terminal experiences a loss of Motorman's indication. If the Conductor's indication is in proper working order, which of the following procedures should the train crew follow?

   A. Continue to operate the train in passenger service only with a Road Car Inspector aboard.
   B. Notify the Command Center and discharge the passengers.
   C. Continue the train in passenger service with the use of buzzer signals.
   D. Discharge the passengers and wait for a Motorman Instructor.

28. When any SMEE type train is stopped in an area where power has been turned off for 30 minutes or more, the hand brakes must be applied on _____ the cars.

   A. at least 1/4 of
   B. at least 1/2 of
   C. at least 3/4 of
   D. all

29. Which of the following statements about R-44 and R-46 type equipment is CORRECT? An _____ -numbered car has _____ cab(s).

   A. even; one
   B. even; two
   C. odd; one
   D. odd; two

30. According to standard flagging rules, movement of a yellow light or flag up and down is a signal to the Motorman to

   A. proceed very slowly and be prepared to stop within range of vision
   B. proceed at a speed of not more than 15 miles per hour
   C. blow his horn and continue at normal speed
   D. proceed normally and expect to find another flagman

31. When a Road Motorman observes smoke ahead, he should

   A. stop his train and operate the nearest emergency alarm box
   B. stop his train and contact the Desk Trainmaster immediately
   C. proceed with caution until fire is observed
   D. stop the train and call the New York City Fire Department

32. The term *impact,* when used with reference to fixed signals along the trackway refers to the

   A. position, form, and color of the signal
   B. color, strength, and form of the signal
   C. form, height, and distance between signal lights
   D. form, weight, and strength of signal lights

33. A Motorman is operating his train in passenger service. The black pointer on the duplex air gauge drops to zero. What should the Motorman do FIRST?

   A. Move the brake handle to the charge position.
   B. Call the Command Center for instructions.

C. Move his brake handle into the emergency position.
D. Leave his cab and walk alongside the train.

34. The brakes are applied in emergency on a crowded 10-car rush hour train. After following school car instructions, the Motorman is ordered by the Command Center to investigate the cause of the *brakes in emergency* (BIE). The Motormans investigation reveals that the tenth car has derailed and some passengers have descended onto the road bed. What should the Motorman do FIRST?

    A. Look for and operate the emergency alarm box.
    B. Persuade passengers to get back into the train.
    C. Call the Command Center and ask for further instructions.
    D. Order the Conductor to call for police assistance.

34._____

35. An 8-track lay-up yard can hold 12 cars on each track.
There are already 5 ten-car trains in this yard.
The number of additional cars that can be stored in this yard is

    A. 36   B. 40   C. 46   D. 60

35._____

36. Twelve trains pass a certain point on a track in the course of one hour.
The headway on that track is _____ minutes.

    A. 3   B. 5   C. 6   D. 8

36._____

37. Opening the trip cock on a subway car in passenger service will result in a(n)

    A. service brake application
    B. brake release
    C. loss of dynamic brake
    D. emergency brake application

37._____

38. A portable train stop is used MAINLY by a

    A. Towerman   B. Motorman Instructor
    C. Conductor   D. Flagman

38._____

39. A Motorman in passenger service should never advance his controller handle to a power position before receiving Motorman's indication.
The MAIN reason for this precaution is to

    A. prevent the train from moving with its doors in open position
    B. prevent the train from taking excess motor power
    C. maintain battery current throughout the train
    D. prevent cars from uncoupling

39._____

40. A Motorman approaches an unlit automatic signal and notices that the tripper is in the clear position.
The Motorman should do which of the following?

    A. Proceed with caution.
    B. Stop and notify the Desk Trainmaster.
    C. Proceed at normal speed.
    D. Wait until he is flagged by a Signal Maintainer.

40._____

KEY (CORRECT ANSWERS)

1. A	11. B	21. A	31. C
2. C	12. C	22. A	32. D
3. C	13. D	23. C	33. D
4. A	14. A	24. A	34. C
5. B	15. A	25. C	35. B
6. D	16. C	26. B	36. B
7. C	17. C	27. D	37. A
8. B	18. C	28. D	38. C
9. A	19. D	29. A	39. B
10. A	20. A	30. B	40. C

EXAMINATION SECTION
TEST 1

DIRECTIONS: Each question or incomplete statement is followed by several suggested answers or completions. Select the one that BEST answers the question or completes the statement. *PRINT THE LETTER OF THE CORRECT ANSWER IN THE SPACE AT THE RIGHT.*

1. If the train whistle becomes inoperative enroute, the train operator should
   A. stop immediately and call the rail control center for orders
   B. operate from the second car
   C. have the conductor blow the whistle when necessary from the cab in his car
   D. proceed cautiously and report the condition at the first opportunity

2. The time when it is LEAST important for local and express trains to make *meets* at transfer points is
   A. late at night
   B. during rush hours
   C. Sunday mornings
   D. Saturday afternoons

3. The round trip time between two terminals, not including layover time, is 1 hour, 20 minutes. A train due to arrive at one terminal at 9:10 should leave the other terminal at
   A. 7:50   B. 8:00   C. 8:10   D. 8:30

4. An express train requires five minutes to make the run between two stations which are two and one-half miles apart. The average speed of the train for this run is _____ MPH.
   A. 24   B. 30   C. 36   D. 42

5. If twenty ten-car trains and ten eight-car trains pass a point on a certain track during one hour, the headway on that track, in minutes, is
   A. 1½   B. 2   C. 3   D. 6

6. One purpose of the electric brake circuit is to
   A. prevent accidental emergency application
   B. apply the brakes equally on all cars at the same time
   C. ensure a smooth final stop under all operating conditions
   D. start all compressors at the same time

7. The signals used at congested stations to permit a train to close in on the train ahead are called _____ signals.
   A. G.T.   B. A.K.   C. S.T.   D. C.I.

8. If a stranger starts to question you about an accident which occurred on the subway, your BEST action in accordance with the rules is to
   A. say "no comment"
   B. ask him for his credentials
   C. refer him to the Transit Authority
   D. answer those questions about which you have first-hand information

9. The assistant dispatcher at a time point requests a train operator to whistle for the signal maintainer when he reaches a particular area. The train operator should
   A. call the rail control center for verification
   B. ask the assistant dispatcher for written authorization
   C. tell the assistant dispatcher that it is a rule violation
   D. acknowledge the request and carry it out

10. Pulling the emergency cord on a subway car
    A. opens an air valve
    B. opens a switch
    C. closes an air valve
    D. closes a switch

11. A passenger on the street at Borough Hall, Brooklyn, requests information as to the most direct means of reaching Herald Square (Broadway and 34th Street, Manhattan). You should tell him to use the _____ Line.
    A. 4th Avenue F train at Jay Street
    B. 7th Avenue
    C. Lexington Avenue
    D. Washington Heights

12. If the electric feature of the electro-pneumatic brake fails to function properly on a moving train, the MOST likely result would be that the train will
    A. make a normal stop when the train operator makes a normal brake application
    B. make an emergency stop when the train operator makes a normal brake application
    C. stop beyond the usual stop when the train operator makes a normal brake application
    D. make a normal stop only if the train operator makes an emergency brake application

13. There is NO rapid transit tunnel under the East River at _____ Street.
    A. 14th   B. 42nd   C. 53rd   D. 67th

14. After coasting for some distance, a train operator on a regular subway run moves the controller handle to multiple and finds that the train does not pick up speed. They CANNOT find out whether the third rail is dead by
    A. turning on the heaters
    B. observing the main car lighting
    C. blowing the train whistle
    D. turning on the fans

15. When operating trains in yards, train operators are instructed to operate from a standing position because, from this position, it is easier to
    A. see anyone near or approaching the track
    B. hold down the handle of the master controller
    C. manipulate the brake handle
    D. see further down the track

16. The Lost and Found Office of the N.Y.C.T.A. is located at
    A. 25 Jamaica Avenue
    B. 3961 10th Avenue
    C. 370 Jay Street
    D. 73 Rockwell Place

17. According to the rules, an employee discovering an incipient fire shall exercise all means in his power to extinguish the fire promptly. An incipient fire means a fire which
    A. is near the third rail
    B. is easy to extinguish
    C. seems to be spreading rapidly
    D. has just started

18. A train operator would be acting in violation of the rules if he
    A. sounded five short blasts of the whistle when skipping a regular passenger station
    B. refused a request to make an extra run after his regular tour
    C. absented himself from duty because of illness
    D. coasted between stations with his reverser centered

19. A train operator taking a lay-up train to the yard, and following a regular passenger train enroute, MUST be especially careful to
    A. follow the train ahead as closely as signals permit
    B. remain outside each passenger station until he can get his entire train beyond it
    C. give the train ahead as much headway as possible without delaying the train behind
    D. keep his speed below 10 MPH at all times

Questions 20-27.

DIRECTIONS: Questions 20 through 27, inclusive, are based on the R-10 or later type passenger cars equipped with ME-42 brake valves.

20. The normal main reservoir pressure is in the range of _____ lbs.
    A. 90 to 105   B. 110 to 120   C. 125 to 150   D. 160 to 180

21. The red hand on the duplex air gage indicates the pressure in the
    A. straight air pipe
    B. brake pipe
    C. brake cylinder
    D. compressor

22. The pressure in the main reservoir is indicated
    A. by the setting of the feed valve
    B. on a gage under one of the seats
    C. on a gage under the car
    D. by the setting of the compressor governor

23. While running in normal service, the red hand of the duplex air gage should read
    A. 0   B. 70   C. 90   D. 110

24. While running in normal service, the black hand of the duplex air gage should read
    A. 0   B. 70   C. 90   D. 110

25. On a properly maintained train, an emergency stop will NOT always result from
    A. operation of the conductor's valve
    B. tripping by an automatic stop
    C. release of the controller handle
    D. rapid decrease in brake pipe pressure

26. Dynamic brakes help the electro-pneumatic brake bring a train to a stop by
    A. allowing the use of larger brake shoes
    B. using a separate set of brake drums
    C. magnetizing the brake shoes
    D. having the driving motors act as a braking force

27. The battery on a train furnishes energy to operate (among other items) the group switches which control the third rail power fed to the main motors. A logical consequence of low battery voltage is, therefore, that
    A. the train may be slow
    B. there may not be enough braking power
    C. arcing may become excessive
    D. the operator may have to notch up the controller by hand

Questions 28-40.

DIRECTIONS: Questions 28 through 40, inclusive, are based on the accompanying illustrations of color-light signals, signs, and markers used on the transit system. A pair of illustrations is given when necessary to show two aspects having the same meaning. In the accompanying illustrations, S denotes an illuminated S sign and W denotes auxiliary white lens illuminated.

28. The indication of this signal is
    A. proceed with caution
    B. stop and then proceed, prepared to stop within vision
    C. proceed with caution at allowable speed
    D. proceed

29. This signal means
    A. proceed with caution
    B. stop and then proceed, prepared to stop within vision
    C. proceed with caution at allowable speed
    D. proceed expecting to find track occupied

30. This signal indicates
    A. stop and stay
    B. stop and then proceed, prepared to stop within vision
    C. proceed with caution at allowable speed
    D. proceed with caution

31. The indication of this illuminated sign is
    A. beginning of time control at indicated speed
    B. speed restricted to indicated speed on curve
    C. take turnout at indicated speed
    D. approaching a terminal, maintain indicated speed

32. This sign means that
    A. there are no speed restrictions beyond this point
    B. you have just passed a length of track signaled for both directions
    C. you have just passed out of interlocking control
    D. block signaling ends at this point

33. This illuminated sign is used as the
    A. station stop marker for 8-car trains
    B. turning point marker for 8-car trains
    C. indication that coasting for an 8-car train should begin here
    D. indication that the rear of an 8-car train is past a crossover

34. This signal aspect means that a train operator may
    A. proceed normally on either route
    B. proceed at not exceeding 25 MPH on main route
    C. proceed normally on diverging route
    D. proceed on main route expecting next signal to be clear

34.____

35. This signal aspect means that a train operator may proceed on
    A. diverging route expecting next signal to be red
    B. main route expecting next signal to be red
    C. diverging route expecting next signal to be clear
    D. main route expecting next signal to be clear

35.____

36. This signal indicates
    A. stop and blow four short blasts
    B. stop, operate stop release, then proceed with caution
    C. stop and stay until a less restrictive aspect appears
    D. stop and telephone for orders

36.____

37. This signal aspect means that an operator may proceed on
    A. diverging route expecting next signal to be red
    B. main route expecting next signal to be red
    C. diverging route expecting next signal to be clear
    D. main route expecting next signal to be clear

37.____

38. The indication shown is proceed
    A. on main route
    B. with caution on diverging route
    C. on diverging route
    D. with caution on main route

38.____

39. The aspect shown means
    A. stop and blow whistle for route
    B. stop, operate stop release, then proceed within vision
    C. stop and stay until a less restrictive aspect appears
    D. stop and telephone for orders

39.____

40. The indication shown would MOST probably permit a train operator to
    A. operate the stop release and then proceed with caution
    B. operate the hand throw switch and then proceed with caution
    C. enter inspection shed with caution
    D. proceed with caution onto yard lead

KEY (CORRECT ANSWERS)

1. A	11. A	21. A	31. A
2. B	12. C	22. C	32. D
3. D	13. D	23. A	33. D
4. B	14. C	24. D	34. D
5. B	15. A	25. C	35. A
6. B	16. C	26. D	36. C
7. C	17. D	27. A	37. C
8. C	18. D	28. D	38. D
9. D	19. B	29. A	39. B
10. A	20. C	30. C	40. D

TEST 2

DIRECTIONS: Each question or incomplete statement is followed by several suggested answers or completions. Select the one that BEST answers the question or completes the statement. *PRINT THE LETTER OF THE CORRECT ANSWER IN THE SPACE AT THE RIGHT.*

1. An IMPORTANT safety concept for a train operator to bear in mind is that
   A. some accidents are unavoidable if the schedule is to be maintained
   B. according to the law of averages, a certain number of accidents will occur each year
   C. some train operators are more apt to have accidents than others
   D. most accidents can be avoided if proper precautions are taken

2. If a train operator has a poor accident record, it would be logical to assume that the train operator is PROBABLY
   A. unlucky   B. careless
   C. overcautious   D. safety conscious

3. Artificial respiration should be started immediately on a train operator who has suffered an electric shock by coming in contact with the third rail if he is
   A. unconscious and breathing heavily
   B. unconscious and not breathing
   C. conscious and in a daze
   D. conscious and badly burned

4. The black hand of the duplex air gage on any type of car indicates the air pressure in the
   A. brake pipe   B. straight air pipe
   C. main air line   D. brake cylinder

5. At blue light locations in the subway, a train operator would expect to find both
   A. emergency alarms and emergency exits
   B. telephones and first aid kits
   C. fire extinguishers and stretchers
   D. telephones and fire extinguishers

6. The SAFEST assumption for a train operator to make when he receives a proceed buzzer signal but his indication light remains dark is that
   A. all side doors are closed   B. the indication lamp has burned out
   C. the indication circuit is defective   D. a side door is open

7. When coupling cars, they should be brought together at a speed of about _____ MPH.
   A. ¼   B. 1   C. 4   D. 7

8. If the headway on a certain track is 5 minutes, the number of trains per hour on that track is
   A. 15   B. 14   C. 12   D. 10

9. If the average speed of a train is 30 miles per hour, the time it takes the train to travel one mile is _____ minute(s).
   A. 1   B. 2   C. 3   D. 4

10. A five-track lay-up yard can hold a total of five ten-car trains. There are already three cars stored on each of four tracks and four cars stored on the fifth track. The number of additional cars that can be stored in this yard is
    A. 14   B. 24   C. 34   D. 44

11. A train operator stops his local train at a home signal indicating Stop. If his train is on an upgrade, the train operator should
    A. apply a light-hand stroke
    B. keep his full service brake applied
    C. graduate off the air brake until the train just begins to roll
    D. apply the brakes in emergency

12. An empty train bound for the yard is halted at a stop signal outside a station occupied by a regular passenger train. According to the rules, the train operator of the empty train should start entering the station
    A. as soon as it is safe to key by the stop signal
    B. as soon as the regular passenger train starts to move
    C. when he is sure to be able to get his entire train into the station
    D. when he is sure to be able to get his entire train past the station

13. Operation of the brake on the latest type of car in use on the transit system has been said to be similar to operation of the brake on an automobile. The GREATEST similarity lies in the fact that
    A. hydraulic brakes are used on both trains and automobiles
    B. the greater the motion of the brake handle or pedal, the harder the brake is applied
    C. both trains and automobiles have foot-operated brakes and hand brakes
    D. there is an individual brake cylinder for each pair of wheels

14. Contact shoe slippers must NOT be used when wet because a wet contact shoe slipper
    A. may adhere to the shoe, causing arcing
    B. is likely to break more easily than a dry one
    C. is not a good insulator, so the user may receive a shock
    D. may wear away rapidly because it is soft

15. To avoid a serious arc, a third rail emergency jumper should NOT be removed from the third rail or shoe until the
    A. main switch is open
    B. shoe is off the third rail
    C. car is in motion
    D. master controller is in the off position

15.____

16. In certain equipment failures it becomes necessary for the operator of a passenger train to operate from the second car with the conductor at the head end to pass back signals via the buzzer. In such cases, the crew is required to discharge passengers at the next station. The BEST reason for discharge of passengers in such cases is that
    A. carrying passengers under these conditions would cause extreme delays
    B. it is not possible to operate safely
    C. incorrect markers are automatically displayed
    D. the train operator cannot see the station stop markers

16.____

Questions 17-21.

DIRECTIONS: Questions 17 through 21, inclusive, are based on the notice given below. Refer to this notice in answering these questions.

NOTICE

Your attention is called to Route Request Buttons that are installed on all new type interlocking home signals where there is a choice of route in the midtown area. The route request button is to be operated by the train operator when the home signal is at danger and no call-on is displayed or when improper route is displayed.

To operate, the train operator will press the button for the desired route as indicated under each button; a light will then go on over the buttons to inform the train operator that his request has been registered in the tower.

If the tower operator desires to give the train operator a route other than the one he selected, the tower operator will cancel out the light over the route selection buttons. The train operator will then accept the route given.

If no route or call-on is given, the operator will sound his whistle for the signal maintainer, secure his train, and call the rail control center.

17. The official titles of the two classes of employee whose actions would MOST frequently be affected by the contents of this notice are
    A. train operator and superintendent
    B. signal maintainer and superintendent
    C. tower operator and train operator
    D. signal maintainer and tower operator

17.____

18. A train operator should use a route request button when
    A. the signal indicates proceed on main line
    B. a call-on is displayed
    C. the signal indicates stop
    D. the signal indicates proceed on diverging route

19. The PROPER way to request a route is to
    A. press the button corresponding to the desired route
    B. press the button a number of times to correspond with the number of the route requested
    C. stop at the signal and blow four short blasts
    D. stop at the signal and telephone the tower

20. The train operator will know that their requested route has been registered in the tower if
    A. a light comes on over the route request buttons
    B. an acknowledging signal is sounded on the tower horn
    C. the light in the route request button goes dark
    D. the home signal continues to indicate stop

21. It is clear that route request buttons
    A. eliminate train delays due to signals at junctions
    B. keep the tower operator alert
    C. force train operators and tower operators to be more careful
    D. are a more accurate form of communication than the whistle

Questions 22-29.

DIRECTIONS: Each of Questions 22 through 29, inclusive, is based on the rule immediately preceding the question. Read the rule carefully before answering the question. Be sure to consider only the information given in the rule immediately preceding the question.

RULE: When a gang or group is going to work under flagging protection at a given location, the office of the Superintendent of Transportation of the division must be notified.

22. Such notification is logically required MAINLY so that
    A. train operators may be alerted
    B. trains may be taken out of service
    C. delays may be avoided
    D. passengers may be informed of possible inconvenience

RULE: The person in charge of the work to be performed shall select the flaggers for each assignment from the list of qualified flagmen established in accordance with instructions of the General Superintendent.

23. This rule CLEARLY implies that
    A. the person in charge of a job trains the flagman or flagmen
    B. nearly all jobs require more than one flagman
    C. there is a list of qualified flagmen available
    D. the work of flagging should be divided equally among the qualified men

RULE: When necessary to signal a train to stop, the employee given such signal must continue to do so until the train has been brought to a stop or the train operator of the train has acknowledged the signal by sounding two short blasts of the whistle.

24. The two short blasts of the whistle are an indication that the
    A. employee giving the stop signal should continue giving the signal
    B. train operator has seen and understood the signal
    C. employee giving the stop signal should step into the clear
    D. train operator has made a full service brake application

25. This rule could NOT apply to _____ signals.
    A. hand   B. flag   C. lantern   D. fixed

RULE: Before coupling cars, train operators must see that the brake is set up on section to which coupling is to be made.

26. The brake is set up to
    A. prevent moving coupled cars with angle cocks closed
    B. make sure that the air lines are properly charged
    C. avoid damage to the couplers
    D. prevent rolling of cars to which coupling is made

RULE: Accident reports, facts, and conditions connected with accidents, and names of witnesses are confidential information. Employees must not communicate either orally or in writing to any person with reference to accidents except to proper officials of the system or except, with knowledge of the Authority, to the proper authorities entitled to such information.

27. The MOST nearly correct statement based on this rule is that
    A. an employee witnessing an accident may give information to system officials only
    B. an employee witnessing an accident should not make any written notes on the accident
    C. the names of witnesses of accidents is confidential information
    D. all accident reports must be given either orally or in writing

28. The MOST probable reason for having this rule is to 28.____
    A. prevent lawsuits
    B. avoid conflicting testimony
    C. prevent unofficial statements from being accepted as official
    D. conceal facts which may be damaging

RULE: In foggy weather or at any time when the train operator's vision is obstructed by snow, rain, sleet, or smoke, etc., they must run the train so that they can stop within range of vision in order to ensure the safety of the train and passengers.

29. This rule means MOST NEARLY that 29.____
    A. the braking distance in snow or sleet storms is about equal to the train operator's range of vision
    B. an train operator's vision is obstructed by fog about as much as it is by smoke
    C. when a train operator's range of vision is reduced, it is generally restricted by fog, snow, rain, sleet, or smoke
    D. if a train operator's view ahead is obstructed, he should operate his train slowly

30. If the motors continue to take power after the train operator of a passenger train has returned the master controller to OFF, his FIRST action in bringing the train back under control should be to 30.____
    A. signal for a car inspector
    B. release the master controller handle
    C. open the control switch
    D. reverse the motors

31. If a speed of 15 miles per hour is exactly 22 feet per second, then the number of miles per hour corresponding to 30 feet per second is MOST NEARLY 31.____
    A. 10   B. 15   C. 20   D. 25

32. If a train operator makes a brake application and holds it without either increasing or graduating off until the train comes to a stop, the result is ALMOST sure to be 32.____
    A. tripping the overload relay   B. overrunning the stop
    C. a hard stop   D. a skid

33. On approaching a home signal indicating STOP in the subway, the train operator observes a white light being moved rapidly up and down alongside the signal. The train operator should 33.____
    A. reduce speed and pass the signal slowly
    B. resume speed and pass the signal normally
    C. stop immediately and telephone for orders
    D. stop at the signal and find out who is waving the light

34. An train operator operating in a yard hears one long blast of the tower whistle. He should
    A. stop his train and await orders or a two-blast horn signal from the tower indicating all clear
    B. increase his speed to clear the switch he is on
    C. slow down to the yard speed limit
    D. continue and be on the watch for the signal maintainer

35. The MOST important reason for coasting as much as possible consistent with keeping on schedule is that this practice reduces
    A. brake shoe wear
    B. contact shoe wear
    C. wheel maintenance
    D. power consumption

36. The normal voltage of the third rail in the subway is NEAREST to _____ volts.
    A. 250
    B. 400
    C. 600
    D. 750

37. A train operator operating their train in customer service approaches a home signal displaying three yellow (amber) lights. The train operator should
    A. stop their train and acknowledge the three yellow (amber) signals with a single horn blast before proceeding at reduced speed and extreme caution
    B. stop their train and contact the rail control center and question this line-up before moving
    C. proceed at a reduced speed using extreme caution expecting to find track personnel on or near the tracks
    D. proceed at normal speed but then reduce speed as they approach the next station expecting to find track personnel on or near the tracks

38. A and C Line trains operating on their normal route utilize which tunnel (tube) into and out of Manhattan?
    A. Montague Street tube
    B. Clark Street tube
    C. York Street tube
    D. Cranberry Street tube

39. A train operator operating their train in customer service was instructed by the rail control center to turn off their air ventilation system because of an odor of smoke. After doing so, this train operator should
    A. make an announcement apologizing for temporarily having to turn off the air ventilation
    B. say nothing to the customers and turn the air ventilation system back on when it is safe to do so
    C. make an announcement that you were instructed to turn off the air ventilation system because of an odor of smoke ahead
    D. say nothing to the customers and turn the air ventilation system on when the rail control center gives you permission

40. Part of a conductor's essential daily equipment is NOT which of the following? 40._____
    A. Rulebook B. Badge
    C. Drum switch key D. Safety vest

KEY (CORRECT ANSWERS)

1.	D	11.	B	21.	D	31.	C
2.	B	12.	D	22.	A	32.	C
3.	B	13.	B	23.	C	33.	D
4.	A	14.	C	24.	B	34.	A
5.	D	15.	D	25.	D	35.	D
6.	D	16.	A	26.	D	36.	C
7.	B	17.	C	27.	C	37.	B
8.	C	18.	C	28.	C	38.	D
9.	B	19.	A	29.	D	39.	B
10.	C	20.	A	30.	C	40.	C

TEST 3

DIRECTIONS: Each question or incomplete statement is followed by several suggested answers or completions. Select the one that BEST answers the question or completes the statement. *PRINT THE LETTER OF THE CORRECT ANSWER IN THE SPACE AT THE RIGHT.*

1. The PROPER way to move a car having inoperative air brakes from a lay-up track into the shop is to operate it slowly
    A. coupled to a car or cars with good brakes
    B. with a slight hand brake applied
    C. using the reverser to stop the car
    D. with a flagman walking ahead

    1.____

2. A train operator in the subway observes a white light moving up and down rapidly some distance ahead of their moving train. If their train has not passed any other warning lantern, the train operator should acknowledge the light with a whistle signal and
    A. stop
    B. reduce speed to 10 MPH
    C. proceed
    D. prepare to stop within range of vision

    2.____

3. Two positions of the master controller which are running positions are
    A. off and switching
    B. switching and series
    C. switching and multiple
    D. series and multiple

    3.____

4. Battery power is used on subway cars to supply energy to the
    A. car heaters
    B. fans
    C. main car lights
    D. emergency lights

    4.____

5. The dead-man feature on subway cars is inoperative whenever the
    A. controller is in the OFF position
    B. brake handle is in the release position
    C. reverser key is centered
    D. reverser key is reversed

    5.____

6. Train operators become acquainted with new regulations MAINLY through
    A. talking to other train operators
    B. school-car instruction
    C. notices posted on bulletin boards
    D. re-issues of the book of rules

    6.____

2 (#3)

7. If an ambulance is required because someone is injured in the subway, train operators are instructed to notify the transit police department and have the transit police call for the ambulance. It is MOST important for the train operators to tell the transit police
   A. where the ambulance is needed
   B. his own name and badge number
   C. whether the injured party is male or female
   D. how severe the injuries are

7.____

Questions 8-20.

DIRECTIONS: Questions 8 through 20, inclusive, are based on the accompanying illustrations of color-light signals, signs, and markers used on the transit system. Since two schemes of signal indication and several forms of sign are in use on the transit system, a pair of illustrations having similar meanings are shown when necessary. In the accompanying illustrations, C O denotes that letters C and O are illuminated, S denotes an illuminated S sign, and (W) denotes auxiliary white lens illuminated.

8. The indication of this signal is
   A. stop and stay
   B. stop and then proceed, prepared to stop within vision
   C. proceed with caution at allowable speed
   D. proceed

8.____

9. This signal indicates
   A. stop and stay
   B. stop and then proceed, prepared to stop within vision
   C. proceed with caution at allowable speed
   D. proceed with caution

9.____

10. The indication of this signal is
    A. proceed with caution
    B. stop and then proceed, prepared to stop within vision
    C. proceed with caution at allowable speed
    D. proceed

10.____

11. This signal means
    A. proceed with caution
    B. stop and then proceed, prepared to stop within vision
    C. proceed expecting to find track occupied

11.____

12. The non-illuminated sign shown means
    A. cut-in power
    B. cut-out lights
    C. car stop
    D. coast

12.____

13. The non-illuminated sign shown is the
    A. station stop marker for 8-car trains
    B. turning point marker for 8-car trains
    C. beginning of coasting marker for 8-car trains
    D. marker for the point at which a 8-car train may resume normal speed

13.____

14. This sign is the
    A. station stop marker for 8-car trains
    B. turning point marker for 8-car trains
    C. beginning of coasting marker for 8-car trains
    D. marker for the point at which an 8-car train may resume normal speed

14.____

15. This illuminated sign is the
    A. station stop marker for 8-car trains
    B. turning point marker for 8-car trains
    C. beginning of coasting marker for 8-car trains
    D. marker for the point at which an 8-car train may resume normal speed

15.____

16. This sign means that
    A. there are no speed restrictions beyond this point
    B. signals beyond this point do not apply to trains
    C. train operators may operate without regard to rules beyond this point
    D. block signaling ends at this point

16.____

17. This signal aspect means switch set for _____ route pass expecting next signal to be _____.
    A. diverging; red
    B. straight; red
    C. diverging; green
    D. straight; green

17._____

18. This signal indicates proceed with caution
    A. into yard
    B. on diverging route
    C. on main route
    D. onto occupied track

18._____

19. The indication shown is
    A. proceed
    B. proceed on diverging route
    C. proceed on main route
    D. proceed with caution

19._____

20. The indication shown would MOST probably permit a train operator to
    A. operate the stop release and then proceed, prepared to stop within vision
    B. operate hand-throw switch and then proceed with caution
    C. enter inspection shed with caution
    D. proceed with caution onto yard lead

20.____

21. This signal aspect means that a train operator may
    A. proceed normally on either route
    B. pass expecting to find next signal on main route yellow or green
    C. proceed on diverging route
    D. proceed at not exceeding 25 MPH on main route

21.____

22. This signal indicates
    A. stop and blow whistle for route
    B. stop, operate stop release, then proceed with caution prepared to stop within range of vision
    C. stop and stay until a less restrictive aspect appears
    D. stop and telephone for orders

22.____

23. The aspect shown means
    A. stop and blow whistle for route
    B. stop, operate stop release, then proceed with caution, prepared to stop within range of vision
    C. stop and stay until a less restrictive aspect appears
    D. stop and telephone for orders

23.____

24. The indication of this illuminated sign is
    A. beginning of time control at indicated speed
    B. speed restricted to 15 MPH on curve
    C. take crossover at 15 MPH
    D. beginning of terminal track; maintain indicated speed

24.____

25. Three short whistle blasts are sounded to
    A. acknowledge a hand signal from someone on the track
    B. warn persons on or near the track to stand clear
    C. call for a transit police officer to meet the train
    D. ask for a car inspector to meet the train

25.____

26. If a subway train goes dead while it is running between stations, the train operator could conclude that the third rail was dead if the
    A. emergency lights in the train were dark
    B. main car lights were dark
    C. train operator's indication light went out
    D. tunnel lights were dark

26.____

27. Normally, when an express train is routed to the local tracks, the train operator is required to stop at
    A. certain specified busy stations only
    B. alternate stations
    C. express stations only
    D. all stations

27.____

28. Any signal imperfectly displayed is to be regarded as the most restrictive indication that can be given by that signal. Accordingly, the indication of an automatic signal which has both the green and yellow lenses illuminated is
    A. proceed with caution
    B. stop and then proceed according to rules
    C. stop and stay and contact the rail control center
    D. proceed with caution at allowable speed

29. A train operator observing the signal of Question 22 above is required by the rules to notify the
    A. superintendent of transportation   B. rail control center
    C. supervisor of signals   D. signal maintainer

30. The train operator of a train stopped in a station notices that there is considerable arcing underneath the car. His BEST initial action is to
    A. whistle for assistance   B. open the main knife switch
    C. contact the rail control center   D. open the control switch

31. The car stop markers for 4-, 5-, 6-, 7-, and 8-car trains at a certain station are located so that a properly stopped train of any length will be centered in the station. The distance between the 5-car and the 8-car stop markers MUST be _____ car lengths.
    A. 3   B. 2½   C. 2   D. 1½

32. Before starting the train to enter a shop building, the train operator MUST
    A. make a brake test   B. set out a warning flag or lantern
    C. sound the proper whistle signal   D. energize the shop third rail

33. A train operator is MOST likely to become aware of a grounded shoe beam on the operating car through the
    A. arcing and acrid odor
    B. tripping of the overload breaker
    C. loss of third rail power
    D. emergency application of the brakes

34. If there is a loss of third rail power and the train operator has permitted the train to coast to a stop between stations, he need NOT necessarily
    A. apply hand brakes   B. leave his cab
    C. telephone the rail control center   D. discharge passengers

35. When coupling cars on a grade, safety requires that the cars moved in making the coupling MUST be
    A. the longer section   B. moved upgrade
    C. the shorter section   D. moved downgrade

36. In making a report of an unusual occurrence on a train in the subway, the LEAST important information to include is
    A. time of day   B. weather
    C. head car number   D. direction of travel

37. Entering a yard lay-up track, the train operator observes a red lantern on the rear of a car at the bumper. His BEST procedure is to
    A. sound his whistle and stop about a foot away
    B. stop a car length away and check with the workers
    C. couple to the car and apply brakes in emergency
    D. stop as soon as he sees the lantern and radio the dispatcher

38. Switch targets or pot signals are used in connection with switches that are operated
    A. pneumatically
    B. electrically
    C. hydraulically
    D. manually

39. Before moving a train in a yard, it is MOST important to check the
    A. brakes
    B. marker lights
    C. couplers
    D. battery

40. One person permitted to ride in the operating cab with the train operator is the
    A. conductor
    B. dispatcher
    C. tower operator
    D. superintendent

KEY (CORRECT ANSWERS)

1. A	11. A	21. B	31. D
2. C	12. D	22. C	32. C
3. D	13. A	23. B	33. A
4. D	14. B	24. A	34. D
5. C	15. D	25. D	35. B
6. C	16. D	26. B	36. B
7. A	17. A	27. C	37. B
8. B	18. C	28. C	38. D
9. C	19. B	29. B	39. A
10. D	20. D	30. C	40. D

TEST 4

DIRECTIONS: Each question or incomplete statement is followed by several suggested answers or completions. Select the one that BEST answers the question or completes the statement. *PRINT THE LETTER OF THE CORRECT ANSWER IN THE SPACE AT THE RIGHT.*

1. In a recent statement by the Transit Authority, their announced surplus was credited MOSTLY to
   A. more riders
   B. reductions in operating personnel
   C. sale of the power houses
   D. new cars and buses

   1._____

2. All train crews must have knowledge of the running time and are also required to know the scheduled time due at principal points and terminals. The MOST logical reason for this requirement is to make
   A. it possible for train crews to be contacted at any time
   B. both the train operator and the conductor responsible for having the train on time at these points
   C. certain that trains never leave principal points later than scheduled
   D. sure that the train crew is able to answer passengers' questions regarding time

   2._____

3. An operating rule states that, when a train is delayed in excess of four minutes for any cause whatsoever, either the train operator or the conductor shall contact the superintendent as soon as possible. The BEST reason for this procedure is so that the
   A. broadcasting companies can be notified of delays in train service
   B. blame for the delay can be properly placed
   C. rail control center can take immediate action
   D. train crew can find out the probable duration of the delay

   3._____

4. Train operators generally know the points at which coasting should be used under normal conditions by
   A. judgment gained through experience
   B. signal indications
   C. signs along the route
   D. bulletins posted at their home terminals

   4._____

5. A *call-on* signal is used only in conjunction with a(n) _____ signal.
   A. automatic   B. dwarf   C. approach   D. home

   5._____

6. Train crews shall be at their operating positions at least two minutes before the schedule time of departure of the train from the terminal. One possible reason for this requirement is that
   A. the train may be dispatched ahead of time in an emergency
   B. a substitute can be assigned in case of no-show
   C. the crew can discuss new bulletin orders
   D. the dispatcher can complete the entry on the sign-on sheet

6._____

7. Third rail power is used to operate the
   A. conductor's signal light
   B. car ventilating fans
   C. train operator's indication light
   D. tail lights

7._____

8. The time interval between trains is known as the
   A. gap
   B. layover time
   C. running time
   D. headway

8._____

9. A proceed hand signal may NEVER be given with a
   A. white light
   B. green lantern
   C. yellow lantern
   D. red lantern

9._____

10. A resume speed signal is a fixed signal located at a point where a train of
    A. any length may resume normal speed after a slow speed move
    B. indicated length, stopped to clear proper switches and signals for a reverse move, may proceed
    C. any length, which is operating in a time-controlled section, may proceed at normal speed
    D. indicated length, which has been running at reduced speed, may resume normal speed

10._____

11. At a blue light location in the subway, you would NOT ordinarily expect to find an emergency
    A. alarm box
    B. telephone
    C. fire extinguisher
    D. exit

11._____

12. Of the following, the one which is NOT a fixed signal is a
    A. coasting sign
    B. yellow lantern hung on a column
    C. slow sign
    D. bumper post light

12._____

13. A color-light signal which is never clear but always displays a red light is a _____ signal.
    A. home
    B. grade time
    C. curve
    D. dwarf marker

13._____

14. When an operator blows three short blasts on the train whistle, he is
    A. signaling for a transit police officer
    B. warning passengers standing too close to the platform edge
    C. calling for the car inspector
    D. acknowledging a lantern signal

14._____

15. According to rules, a subway train may move over a crossover for which no speed limiting sign is displayed at a MAXIMUM speed of _____ MPH.
    A. 8   B. 10   C. 12   D. 15

16. One function of the emergency alarm system in the subway is to
    A. remove power from the third rail
    B. supply power to the car emergency lights
    C. provide a means of communication in the event of a power failure
    D. sound a warning in the nearest transit police office

Questions 17-20.

DIRECTIONS: Questions 17 through 20, inclusive, are based on the rule immediately preceding each question. Be sure to consider only the information given in the rule for each question.

RULE: Accident reports, facts, and conditions connected with accidents and names of witnesses are confidential information. Employees must not communicate either orally or in writing to any person with reference to accidents except to proper officials of the system or except, with knowledge of the Authority, to anyone entitled to such information.

17. The MOST likely reason for this rule is to
    A. avoid conflicting testimony
    B. prevent lawsuits
    C. conceal facts which may be damaging
    D. prevent unofficial statements from being accepted as official

RULE: When operating a light train on the main line, train operators must never enter a station until they can get the entire train beyond the station.

18. According to this rule, a train operator operating a light train held out of a local station by an entering automatic signal which is red, may start to enter the station when he sees that the
    A. entering automatic signal has changed to yellow
    B. station area is clear of the train ahead
    C. leaving automatic signal has changed to yellow
    D. train in the station has started to move

RULE: Employees required to work on or adjacent to tracks in the subway must not begin work on the track in any way without first displaying signal lights as follows:
Two lighted yellow lanterns approximately 500 feet in advance of the point of work;
A lighted red lantern not less than 75 feet in advance of the work;
A lighted green lantern at a safe distance beyond the work.

19. In this rule, a safe distance means MOST likely that the green lantern should be placed
    A. a train length past the yellow lights
    B. 75 feet past the red light
    C. a train length past workers on the track
    D. 500 feet past the yellow lights

RULE: Operators must not run ahead of schedule time unless ordered to do so by proper authority.

20. The MOST likely reason for this rule is based on the fact that trains running ahead of schedule
    A. have to be held at time points to get them back on schedule
    B. use more power as they do less coasting
    C. cause the train following to become overloaded and delayed
    D. disrupts the routine of employees working on tracks between train intervals

21. If an train operator receives a poorly executed hand or lantern signal so that they are not positive of the meaning, the BEST action for them to follow would be to
    A. assume the most likely meaning
    B. proceed cautiously
    C. stop immediately
    D. disregard the signal entirely

22. Of the following actions of a train operator, the one which would NOT be considered a violation of the rules would be to
    A. come to work without his watch
    B. stop his train in a station a car length beyond the car stop marker
    C. operate in regular passenger service with his cab door open
    D. sound several blasts of the whistle when skipping a regular passenger station

23. The rules state that, on straight yard track, the MAXIMUM speed at which the train may be operated is
    A. series   B. switching   C. multiple   D. 20 MPH

24. The PROPER speed at which cars should be brought together when coupling is nearest to _____ feet per _____.
    A. 2; second   B. 10; second   C. 2; minute   D. 10; minute

25. If in doubt as to the meaning of any rule, regulation, or instruction, the BEST procedure for a train operator to follow is to
    A. ask another train operator for an explanation
    B. obtain an explanation from the dispatcher
    C. use his own best judgment when a situation arises
    D. discuss the matter with his conductor

26. Sometimes conductors in passenger service close train doors without properly observing passengers entering or leaving the train. This is an improper action CHIEFLY because
    A. the conductor might strike a passenger with a closing door
    B. an exiting passenger might be left on the train
    C. passengers who hold doors open cannot be seen
    D. a passenger might be left on the platform

27. The protection of the *dead-man* feature on a moving train is lost when the
    A. train is coasting   B. brakes are applied in emergency
    C. reverser is centered   D. electric brake is not cut in

28. Single-track operation is generally necessary when
    A. a train with locked brakes blocks a main line
    B. signal cables are being replaced in an under-river tunnel
    C. running rails are being renewed in an express station
    D. lightbulbs are being replaced in an under-river tunnel

29. Unless the braking pressure is gradually reduced as the train nears a stop, the result will MOST likely be
    A. a hard stop   B. over-running the stop
    C. constant deceleration   D. a danger of skidding

30. A rule of the Transit Authority is that any employee must give his name and badge number when requested by a passenger
    A. only if a valid reason is given
    B. without delay or argument
    C. only if the passenger is insistent
    D. without argument, but only after first trying to placate the passenger

31. The law requires that subway cars in passenger service during the winter season must be kept heated between 40 and 65 degrees. It is MOST likely that these particular limits were picked because they
    A. result in minimum fogging of windows
    B. are the most comfortable year-round temperatures
    C. are most economical
    D. are comfortable for passengers wearing outdoor clothing

32. The LEAST valuable source for improvements in operating procedures is the
    A. suggestions of employees
    B. working agreement
    C. letters from passengers
    D. dispatcher's records

33. A six-track lay-up yard can hold twelve cars on each track, but there are already four ten-car trains in this yard. The number of additional cars that can be stored in this yard is
    A. 12   B. 32   C. 40   D. 72

34. A train operator, operating in a yard, hearing one long blast on the tower whistle, knows that the tower operator is signaling for
    A. all trains in the yard to come to an immediate stop
    B. the dispatcher to come to the tower
    C. a train on the yard leads to enter the yard
    D. the signal maintainer to call his field office

35. A train operator shows up to work smelling of alcohol but has NOT yet signed on to work. The FIRST duty of the supervisor is to
    A. send this employee to the transit clinic for substance abuse testing
    B. allow this employee to sign on the payroll and then immediately send them for substance abuse testing
    C. contact the area superintendent and the rail control center
    D. send the employee home immediately

KEY (CORRECT ANSWERS)

1.	A	11.	D	21.	C	31.	D
2.	B	12.	B	22.	D	32.	B
3.	C	13.	D	23.	A	33.	B
4.	C	14.	C	24.	A	34.	A
5.	D	15.	B	25.	B	35.	C
6.	A	16.	A	26.	A		
7.	B	17.	D	27.	C		
8.	D	18.	C	28.	B		
9.	D	19.	C	29.	A		
10.	D	20.	C	30.	B		

TEST 5

DIRECTIONS: Each question or incomplete statement is followed by several suggested answers or completions. Select the one that BEST answers the question or completes the statement. *PRINT THE LETTER OF THE CORRECT ANSWER IN THE SPACE AT THE RIGHT.*

1. Train operators' reporting times are usually 10 to 15 minutes before their trains are scheduled to depart. Of the following, the LEAST important reason for this time interval is to allow the train operator to
    A. change into his working clothes
    B. check the condition of his train
    C. check that his conductor has signed in
    D. take care of any personal needs

2. A train operator taking a lay-up train over the road to a yard
    A. must operate from a standing position
    B. may not exceed 10 MPH at any time
    C. may follow the train ahead of him as close as safety permits
    D. must observe certain special rules

3. The position to which the master controller handle has been moved by the train operator determines the
    A. braking power available
    B. availability of the *dead-man*'s feature
    C. maximum speed to which the train may accelerate

4. When a train operator's indication light is illuminated, it is an indication that
    A. all brakes are released
    B. the third rail is alive
    C. all side doors are closed and locked
    D. the main car fuse is okay

5. The type of signal used at congested stations to *close-in* trains is known as a _____ signal.
    A. repeater   B. station time
    C. grade time   D. train order

6. It is generally true that the principal cause of MOST accidents is
    A. fatigue   B. physical disability
    C. carelessness   D. sabotage

7. The BEST way for a train operator to acquaint themselves with new regulations as soon as possible is to
    A. study the book of rules
    B. depend on specific notice by the train service supervisor
    C. be alert to the needs of the service
    D. read all bulletins as issued

8. Loss of third rail power on a subway car will FIRST prevent functioning of the
   A. air compressor
   B. train whistle
   C. service brakes
   D. pneumatically operated doors

9. Timetables are often made up so that both local and express trains are scheduled to arrive at a station at the same time in order to afford passengers an opportunity to change trains. From the passengers' viewpoint, it is MOST important for timetables to be so made up when the
   A. headways are short
   B. express stations are far apart
   C. local and express trains are bound for different terminals
   D. headways are long

10. Train operators are required to coast as much as possible consistent with running on time. The MOST important reason for coasting is that it reduces
    A. wheel maintenance
    B. brake shoe wear
    C. power consumption
    D. contact shoe arcing

11. A facing point switch is a switch the points of which
    A. face in the direction of traffic flow
    B. make up against the face of rail
    C. face approaching traffic
    D. face the tower

12. Trains of two converging routes approach a junction at the same time. It is logical to assume that the train which should go FIRST is the one which
    A. does arrive first
    B. is carrying the greater passenger load
    C. has the greater number of cars
    D. is scheduled to arrive first

13. If the running time between the two towers at the ends of a certain tunnel is 3½ minutes, the MINIMUM headway in one direction when single-tracking is operated is _____ minutes.
    A. 3½   B. 7   C. 10½   D. 14

14. A train operator should be particularly alert to guard against sliding the wheels on a yard track
    A. when the rails have been renewed
    B. during a long dry spell
    C. at the beginning of a light rain
    D. immediately after the rails have been polished

15. The purpose of a contact shoe slipper is to
    A. simplify the removal of a badly worn contact shoe
    B. insulate the contact shoe from the third rail
    C. make the shoe slid easily on the third rail
    D. ensure good contact with the third rail

16. A train operator, operating a train in regular service, observes three lighted yellow lanterns displayed alongside of his track. The train operator should
    A. slow down and sound one long and one short whistle blast
    B. slow down and sound two short whistle blasts
    C. proceed normally
    D. stop for instructions from the first flagman

17. Opening the trip cock on a subway car will ordinarily result in
    A. an emergency brake application
    B. the electric brake becoming inoperative
    C. a service brake application
    D. releasing the brakes

18. When a train operator is reporting a fire by phone, it would be LEAST important for them to report
    A. the time when he noticed the fire
    B. the location of the fire
    C. his name and pass number
    D. the nature of the trouble

19. When the train operator of a passenger train descends to the track to the track to check his train because the brakes fail to release, he need NOT
    A. take the reverser key with him
    B. set up a hand brake
    C. inform the conductor
    D. pull the emergency alarm

20. During the time when 15 trains pass a certain point on one track in one hour, the headway on that track, in minutes, is
    A. 2   B. 4   C. 8   D. 15

21. An express train requires five minutes to make the run between two stations which are two miles apart. The average speed of the train, in miles per hour, for this run is
    A. 20   B. 24   C. 30   D. 36

22. Hand brakes are to be set up on three cars of a ten-car train laid up on a grade. If the cars are numbered 1 to 10 starting with the car that is highest on the grade, it would be BEST to set up the hand brakes on
    A. cars 1, 2, and 3
    B. cars 2, 5, and 9
    C. cars 8, 9, and 10
    D. any three cars

23. After applying the required number of hand brakes on a train which has been laid up on a grade, the PROPER test of whether the hand brakes will hold the train is to
    A. examine each hand brake chain to see that it is right
    B. apply the brakes in emergency
    C. place the brake valve in release
    D. apply one point of power to see if the train will move

24. The term *automatic stop*, as used on the transit system, means a
    A. device used by a conductor to apply the brakes in emergency
    B. device on the roadway which applies the brakes when a train passes a red signal
    C. scheduled stop for an express operating on the local track
    D. train stop which is initiated by the train operator

25. Unused sections of track should be operated over at more or less regular intervals to make sure that
    A. any rust on the rails will be worn off
    B. the roadbed is being properly maintained
    C. no obstructions have been placed in the path of a train
    D. the switches are in good operating condition

26. A train operator, operating a train in regular service, sees an individual step out of the way of the train and wave a green lantern up and down. The train operator should
    A. sound two short whistle blasts and proceed normally
    B. sound a succession of short whistle blasts and proceed normally
    C. stop for identification of the individual
    D. proceed normally with no whistle response

27. If a transit employee saw a passenger knocked down on the station platform by another passenger who was rushing to the train, the FIRST action to be taken by the employee should be to
    A. ascertain if the passenger was injured
    B. get the names of witnesses
    C. report the incident to the transit police
    D. obtain the passengers' names and addresses

28. Three green lightbulbs at a terminal positioned nearest the conductor's position when illuminated tell the conductor to
    A. keep train doors open for a connection with an arriving train
    B. close down doors and notify the train operator to proceed
    C. secure train and report to the dispatcher's office
    D. make all local stops

29. A repeater signal is MOST usually found on
    A. elevated structures   B. curves
    C. yards   D. leaving terminals

30. The three MAIN radio frequencies used by subway personnel are
    A. B1, B2, and C1   B. A division, B1, and B2
    C. A1, A2, and B division   D. 101, 102, and 103

KEY (CORRECT ANSWERS)

1.	C	11.	C	21.	B
2.	D	12.	D	22.	C
3.	C	13.	B	23.	C
4.	C	14.	C	24.	B
5.	B	15.	B	25.	A
6.	C	16.	B	26.	A
7.	D	17.	A	27.	A
8.	A	18.	A	28.	B
9.	D	19.	D	29.	B
10.	C	20.	B	30.	B

www.ingramcontent.com/pod-product-compliance
Lightning Source LLC
Chambersburg PA
CBHW082213300426
44117CB00016B/2791